Praise for *Age in Place*

"With both wit and wisdom, Lynda imparts invaluable strategies and tips to help seniors safely remain in their homes."

—Michael Leonard Wolff, MD, FACP, Program Director, Geriatric Medicine Fellowship, Albany Medical College; Professor, Ringel Institute of Gerontology; Chief Physician, Continuing Care, St. Peter's Health Partners, Albany, New York

"Age in Place *is a godsend for family caregivers wondering if their aging parents are safe in their home. Filled with practical tips and easily implemented strategies, Lynda Shrager's engaging book is a pleasure to read. Give this book to every person you know who has an aging parent!*"

—Amy S. D'Aprix, MSW, PhD, Life Transition Expert, Internationally renowned expert on lifestyle issues related to aging

"Lynda Shrager shares her extensive knowledge, pragmatic know-how, and empathic perspective about one of the most challenging questions many adult children need to ask themselves when it comes to their aging parents . . . 'What do we do now?' When a parent's health fails them but their resistance to move doesn't, Lynda helps the reader understand his or her parent's perspective. She also skillfully assists her readers to manage this challenging and often emotionally draining issue, while making sure the aging parent continues to feel loved, respected, and safe. It's a must-read for anyone facing this overwhelming, yet very common, situation."

—Dr. Robi Ludwig, TV host/personality, author, and psychotherapist

Age in Place

*A Guide to Modifying, Organizing, and
Decluttering Mom and Dad's Home*

Keep Them Safe, Keep YOU Sane

Lynda G. Shrager

Occupational Therapist, Social Worker,
Certified Aging in Place Specialist

aka *The Organized Caregiver*

Bull Publishing Company

Published by Bull Publishing Company
P.O. Box 1377
Boulder, CO, USA 80306
www.bullpub.com

Library of Congress Cataloging-in-Publication Data

Names: Shrager, Lynda G., author.

Title: Age in place : a guide to modifying, organizing and decluttering mom and dad's home keep them safe, keep you sane / Lynda G. Shrager, Occupational Therapist, Social Worker, Certified Aging in Place Specialist, aka The Organized Caregiver.

Description: Boulder, CO : Bull Publishing Company, [2018] | Includes bibliographical references and index.

Identifiers: LCCN 2017057144 | ISBN 9781945188183 (alk. paper)

Subjects: LCSH: Older people--Dwellings--Safety measures. | Barrier-free design for older people.

Classification: LCC NA7195.A4 S57 2018 | DDC 720/.47--dc23

LC record available at https://lccn.loc.gov/2017057144

Printed in USA

23 22 21 20 19 18   10 9 8 7 6 5 4 3 2 1

Interior design and project management: Dovetail Publishing Services
Cover design and production: Shannon Bodie, BookWise Design

To my husband, Steven, who has read every single word I have put down on the page and helped me to rework it until we got it right.

There were so many times I wanted to throw in the towel, and without your constant support and encouragement this book would never have come to fruition. I love you for always seeing the positive and never letting me give up my determination to complete this project.

In preparation for aging in place with you, I have already researched walkers that traverse the sand and an all-terrain beach buggy that goes right into the ocean. We will be ready.

Contents

This book is as accurate as its publisher and authors can make it, but we cannot guarantee that it will work for you in every case. The authors and publisher disclaim any and all liability for any claims or injuries that you may believe arose from following the recommendations set forth in this book. This book is only a guide; your common sense, good judgment, and partnership with health professionals are also needed.

Acknowledgments

Thank you:

To my parents, Joan and Donald Goldstein. You both died so young but thankfully never had to leave the home you held so dear. You were and always will be an inspiration to me.

To my patients for the opportunity to come into your homes and share my expertise with you. Helping you to safely navigate while achieving your independence has given me the unique perspective to write this book. Sharing your insights and techniques for making it work as you age in your home has been truly enlightening for me. I may have been your therapist, but so many times you were the teachers and I was the student.

To the families of my patients who have incorporated my recommendations into your repertoire of strategies to deal with mom and dad and who have shared your ideas and best practices with me. You have indeed become organized caregivers.

To Barbara Lombardo, editor extraordinaire. Your expertise in your field is amazing. Thank you so much for formulating my first draft into a polished manuscript before I ever handed it in.

To Jim Bull for having faith in me and knowing when to reject my early submissions and let me down easy while simultaneously giving me the encouragement and knowledge I needed to finally get it right.

To Emily Sewell—Your unwavering patience and ability to facilitate the back and forth between the cover designer and me was appreciated. Because we all know, you can and will judge a book by its cover.

To Claire Cameron—Since 2011 when we first made contact you opened the door to making this entire project a reality. Your constant calming presence, unwavering support, and quick response time to my endless questions is appreciated more than you'll ever know.

To Jon Ford—the best copyeditor ever. Your ability to point out mistakes and make gentle corrections while not making the writer feel inadequate is a gift.

To Jon Peck—Your ability to turn thousands of words on a computer into a beautifully finished "real" book is amazing.

To Diane Cohen—my physical therapy friend, partner in crime, and story sharer. You are my witness to the fact that you can't make this stuff up.

And last but certainly not least to my beautiful daughters Leslie and Samantha. Thank you for letting me roll ideas off your backs, providing feedback as this book evolved and being there as my first line cheerleaders. I love you both so much.

By the way—dad and I will be aging at the beach.

Introduction

"I'm just warning you, the only way I am leaving this house is horizontally."

My new 92-year-old, 95-pound patient stood guarding her front doorway with her walker. I had just introduced myself as the occupational therapist from the agency assigned to her case. Josie was angry at her kids for insisting she have home care after her hospitalization for a hip fracture that resulted from a fall.

"I don't blame you," I said. "This is a great house. How long have you lived here?"

Her demeanor softened a bit and she allowed me through the entrance. "My husband built it over sixty years ago. The children were born and raised here. John died three years ago and I've managed just fine since then."

"So what happened?"

"I had a little fall in the bathroom. To tell you the truth I don't remember what happened. One minute I was up and the next I was down. The kids are mad that I didn't press the Lifeline, but it was very late and I didn't want to bother anyone. So I lay there all night. My daughter found me in the morning. Now they are throwing ideas around about assisted living or me going to live with one of them. Over my dead body!"

After more than thirty-seven years working in the field of geriatrics, thirteen of them in direct home care, I have experienced hundreds of versions of that conversation. The actors are different; the script is the same. Mom and/or dad have lived in their home for a long time. They are starting to have difficulty getting around and managing the daily requirements of maintaining a house. The decline is often so slow that every minuscule loss of function just becomes the new norm, and they adapt well enough so it doesn't cause a problem. That is until a fall or a new health issue sends them spiraling and exacerbates their functional losses, and before anyone knows what hit them they have a crisis on their hands.

That's when I get the frantic phone call.

"My mom is recovering from pneumonia and is so weak she can't get off the toilet. What do I do?"

"Dad was outside doing yard work and the neighbor called to tell me he had trouble getting up his front steps. What do I do?"

"Mom fell getting out of the tub and was sprawled out on the floor all night with what ended up to be a hip fracture. My sister flew in and is staying with her until she heals, but we are not sure she can stay home alone anymore. I am about to go on a two-month sabbatical to Japan. What should we do?"

"My dad's dementia has gotten so bad he doesn't recognize any of his kids or grandchildren. He knows my mother is someone special to him but he does not know she is his wife. He needs twenty-four-hour supervision and we are afraid Mom will burn out. She insists on keeping him home, and all three of us kids live out of state with families and jobs. What do we do?"

"Our parents are driving us crazy. Mom is literally teetering around the house with her cane trying to cook and clean, and we know she is stiff and in pain from her arthritis. Dad can barely get up from his favorite chair where he sits all day watching TV. His drastic loss of hearing hinders his conversations with Mom and he often yells at her out of frustration. They are both an accident waiting to happen. What do we do?"

The answer to "what do we do" requires that everyone tries to see the situation through their loved ones' eyes, with respect, and that everyone gives a little. That's where this book comes in.

When the issue of "How safe is mom or dad?" and "Can they stay in their home?" arises, it often causes a conflict between the kids and the parents. It's natural to view the situation through our own lens, thus creating different and sometimes clashing versions of the same reality. My experience reveals that most of the time the parents are not being purposefully argumentative. We often picture ourselves as the same as when we were young, ignoring signs of aging that have become part of our everyday life. We discount that pain in our backs when we lift something heavy or the twinge in our knee when we go up the stairs. We overlook the fact that our energy level isn't the same as it used to be and continue to plow on through our day. It's the same with mom and dad, who likely are at least twenty years older than "us kids." The years have taken a toll on their physical and cognitive abilities, but if it's come on slowly they probably didn't notice it happening.

As much as you are sure they are not totally safe and they are having difficulty getting around the house and managing, mom and dad are thoroughly convinced they are fine. And as much as you plead and cajole them to make some changes, in the end it is their right to dismiss your suggestions, recommendations, pleadings, and threats.

So how do you resolve this conflict?

The answer is to somehow meet in the middle. Make a deal. Get them to agree to modify their surroundings so they *can* stay home, but in a living environment that is more accessible, safer, and easier to successfully navigate. This book will show you how to do exactly that, reducing everyone's stress level and hopefully leading to a resolution that makes everyone happy.

Remember, your parents are grown-ups and have managed to do a pretty good job progressing to where they are today. They deserve independence, autonomy, and respect. And they, in turn, need to be open to suggestions that will improve chances for preventing falls and promoting safer mobility in and out of their home. Everyone has to give a little. Use this book as the facilitator to get you all through the process to an effective outcome.

Age in Place: A Guide to Modifying, Organizing, and Decluttering Mom and Dad's Home is a step-by-step, room-by-room guide to simple and often immediate modifications that can help seniors make their homes safer and easier to navigate. AARP (formerly known as the

American Association of Retired Persons) states that "more than 90% of seniors prefer to age in place; staying in their own homes, continuing to make independent choices and maintaining control over their lives."[1] This book will guide these seniors and you, their caregivers and loved ones, on how best to modify their environment so that they can safely and successfully move around and access all areas of the home.

Since we're on the subject of who this book is guiding, let's talk about the audience for *Age in Place*. A large segment of our senior population is quite capable of taking the advice contained herein and independently making numerous adjustments, modifications, and renovations to help themselves age in place. Although the language of this book is directed toward caregivers, it is my hope and expectation that many seniors will pick up this book as well and proactively work toward improving their own situation without bothering the "kids."

That said, many of the people in this age group that I have worked with over the years are reluctant to admit that living in their home has become increasingly difficult. Most often they will not initiate any significant life changes, so it will be up to those who care for them and provide support to get the ball rolling. So where you read "kids," that covers all of us baby boomers, Gen Xers, and those approaching that age group. When you read "mom and dad," that covers who we are ultimately trying to help with this book. It could also be your grandparents, aunts and uncles, or any elderly people in your life. The goal is to help any senior person who is trying to live life to the fullest remain in their own home and successfully age in place.

In part 1, join me on a guided residential walking tour starting with the exterior (sidewalk, driveway, and lawn), through the entranceway, and into the living room, kitchen, bathrooms, bedrooms, laundry area, hallways, stairs, basement, and garage. Along the way I'll discuss flooring, positioning of furniture, appliances, lighting, faucets, even door handles and how best to make modifications to maximize ease of use.

I will also provide decluttering and organizing tips for each room. An orderly and well-maintained house is a safe house. To maximize health and safety, it is helpful to start with decluttering. Clutter takes up precious space and can actually be hazardous to your parents' health. It accumulates excess dust and makes it harder to move around the house safely. And the disorganization contributes to stress by making us feel out of control.

Occupational therapists (lovingly called "OTs" for short) are experts in studying the ease and safety in which their patients perform self-care activities. These activities are called "activities of daily living" (ADLs) or "instrumental activities of daily living" (IADLs). ADLs and IADLs are anything people do from the minute they wake up in the morning until they go to bed at night. This includes feeding oneself, dressing, bathing, toileting, grooming, hygiene, and functional mobility (walking and transferring from surface to surface). IADLs are a bit more complicated in that they include making meals, shopping, managing medications and transportation, and managing the home. As we proceed from room to room, we will discuss how best to maximize mom and dad's ability to safely perform needed ADLs and IADLs.

At the end of each chapter in part 1 there are "Hacks for Health and Home," where I share occupational therapy tips gathered from more than thirty-seven years of working in the field of geriatrics and more than thirteen years working with seniors in their homes.

In part 2, I will explain how family members can best organize their efforts to care for mom and dad. This includes how to detect indicators that help is needed in the house, strategies to encourage parents to accept help, methods to organize both the caregiving team and the tasks that need to be undertaken, and the secret of creating the all-important "command central."

Peppered throughout parts 1 and 2 are photographs of modifications and recommendations for the best home medical equipment, along with explanations for its appropriate use. You'll also find numerous recommendations for where to obtain referenced services as well as additional helpful resources.

Part 3 educates the reader on what important documents need to be organized so they can be easily retrieved. Having to scramble to find your parents' important papers in a crisis only adds more stress to the situation at hand. Organizing the information and being able to easily retrieve it will prove to be invaluable.

Many seniors desire to remain in their homes where they raised their families and created so many wonderful memories, but those desires are often derailed by declining physical and cognitive abilities. As we age we must adapt to the challenges of performing the activities of daily living that we used to take for granted, such as climbing stairs, bathing, preparing meals, and managing the house. Intellectually, we know that being proactive and planning ahead is the way to achieve the best possible results.

Even with the best of intentions, we are often unsure how to start the process, which results in the situation managing us instead of the other way around. *Age in Place: A Guide to Modifying, Organizing, and Decluttering Mom and Dad's Home* is designed to help seniors and their caregivers address these new challenges together, to make life at home safer and more manageable.

I often hear the analogy when dealing with senior parents that now "we" have become the parents and they have become the "kids." Sometimes we lose sight of the impact our parents have had on our entire life. We may have taught them how to use a smartphone or Skype with their grandchildren, but let's not forget that they taught us hygiene, manners, and basic life skills. Remember that your best chance for success is to work cooperatively with mom and dad, not to lose your patience, and to always treat them with the respect they deserve. It's a win-win. They'll be safe. You'll be sane.

Part 1

Declutter and Modify—Ins and Outs

CHAPTER 1

The Exterior

Antonio said: I am an 87-year-old man who has been the primary caretaker for my wife, Maria, who suffers with dementia. My daughter describes me as proud and stubborn. I refer to myself as independent. My wife was recently admitted to a long-term care facility and I have been living on my own for several months. One day while I was tending to my tomato plants on the side of the house, I fell into a ditch that had formed by the runoff of rainwater from the roof. It must have been caused by my clogged gutters that I have not had a chance to clean out. I lay there for what seemed like half a day until my neighbor thankfully found me. He insisted on calling an ambulance to take me to the hospital, although I was sure I was okay. Nothing was broken, but I will admit to feeling very sore and fairly weak. I am very sad that my wife is dying and I realize that I will be alone permanently. My daughter, who lives two hours away, has been staying with me since the fall to help with household tasks and also to make end-of-life arrangements for my wife.

The daughter said: I have told my father a hundred times that the lawn becomes dangerous after a heavy rain and he needs to be very cautious when walking out to his tomatoes. It's a wonder he didn't climb the ladder to clean out the gutters, which he has been known to do. He insists on doing all of the household chores plus the home maintenance. He is determined to go down to the basement to do his laundry and I am petrified he will fall down the stairs.

My stress level is very high right now as my mom's health is failing quickly, Dad is depressed, and although he refuses to admit it, I think he is scared to be totally alone. My two daughters and husband are two hours away, and the running back and forth is starting to weigh on me.

I have hired a private aide and although Dad is against it, I am going to insist she come several days a week to help with the laundry and other things that need to get done.

Lynda said: I had been the occupational therapist for Antonio's wife, Maria, about a year prior and had noted then that he was in great condition for his age. Imagine my surprise when he was assigned to me as a new patient. My assessment included his physical and cognitive levels plus his ability to navigate both outside and inside his home. As soon as he got home, Antonio desired to start doing daily activities again, including picking fresh vegetables from his garden to make sauce and going down the steep basement stairs to do his laundry. Antonio's daughter was distraught thinking he would fall again and needing to return home as soon as possible to tend to her own family.

I created an exercise program and instructed Antonio in carrying it out to improve his overall strength, balance, and mobility while at the same time teaching him techniques to safely complete his activities of daily living (ADLs) and instrumental activities of daily living (IADLs).

His daughter hired a landscaper to repair the outside topography and someone to clean out the gutters. She then set him up with a personal emergency response system with a GPS so Antonio could walk around his property with peace of mind—at least for his daughter. He agreed to have the aide three times a week to do the heavy cleaning and the laundry until he was able to demonstrate to me that he was safe going down to the basement. (See chapter 7 for tips on laundry in the basement.) Once this was all in place, his daughter returned home to her family.

The Exterior

Enjoying one's home should include the property that surrounds it. Whether that is a postage stamp–sized patch of grass, three acres of rolling hills, woods leading to a stream, or a sidewalk melding into a city street, we should strive for safe and easy mobility. When helping mom and dad to stay safely in their home, start by checking out the exterior.

Walkways

When considering the outside of the house, start by evaluating the condition of the driveway and sidewalks. This is an often neglected aspect of the property, especially if the homeowner has become relatively homebound and does not venture outside a lot. Walkways should be checked for cracks, loose bricks or pavers, and holes that have developed over time. Slate and brick sidewalks can become warped as the earth shifts, causing dips that can be dangerous. If you note these problems, consider repaving or at least fixing the trouble spots.

Bannisters or handrails are not just for the staircase in front or back of the house. A handrail can be constructed to go along the walkways leading out to the backyard or along the sidewalk and out to the driveway. They can be incorporated into planters or blended in with shrubs that are maintained at the correct height. If there are lengthy sidewalks or walking paths throughout the property, placing benches at intervals provides a place to rest and break up the "journey."

Install sufficient lighting along pathways. Floodlights with motion sensors that detect when a person or animal approaches the house are a great safety feature and help immeasurably when going out at dusk or after dark.

If mom and dad live in a part of the country where snow and ice are prevalent, it is imperative that walkways are kept clear and deiced. After many years of living in the same home, resurfacing or replacing the sidewalk may be needed, and you might consider installing heat-producing coils that can prevent snowpack and ice from forming. These snow-melting systems are gaining more widespread use in residential housing. Remember, too, that fallen leaves will make their walk slippery and need to be removed.

Don't neglect the walkways leading to an unattached garage or any other type of outbuilding. They should be kept clear of stones and twigs and maintained in the same way as the sidewalks leading to the house. Adequate lighting again is essential.

Driveways

Many of us have found ads stuck in our screen door from driveway sealer companies offering a "great deal" because they are in the neighborhood doing everyone else's driveway. Although it is necessary to maintain the surface of the driveway, seal-coating it every few years can cause the driveway to become slick and slippery. One patient of mine fell and broke her hip as she walked to the mailbox at the end of her newly resealed driveway. Two years later I was assigned to the same house, this time to treat the husband who had fractured his hip in exactly the same way—walking to get the mail two days after they had resealed the driveway.

If mom or dad's driveway is resealed, remind them to take great care when walking on it for the first few weeks until it gets roughed up a bit. For added safety, prior to resealing, discuss with the service provider the possibility of mixing in a product with the chosen material that could give the surface some added traction. Walkways, patios, and decks can also be redone using special products that create nonslip surfaces.

Lawns

There is no such thing as a perfectly flat lawn. There will always be dips and undulations, or actual ditches as in Antonio's case. The best that you can do is take a walk throughout your parents' property at least a few times a year to look for potential problem areas (change of seasons is a good time if you geographically have them). If you find any, especially in places that are regularly traveled, take action to repair or at least mark them in some way so they can be avoided. A tall garden stake with a decorative top placed right in the problem area will warn walkers of potential hazards. If the backyard is hilly or you are concerned about unexpected dips, suggest they use a walking stick or trekking poles to increase safety when walking around the yard. Several of my patients use these for walking in their neighborhoods in all types of weather. For a visual on these products to aid in keeping one's balance, search "trekking poles" on YouTube.

Outdoor Activities

Your evaluation of the walkways, driveway, and lawn of your parents' home should naturally extend to the activities they perform while they're out enjoying or maintaining these areas.

Gardening

Many of my patients take a great deal of pride in their gardens. Although gardening is an activity that inherently offers many benefits, such as relaxing the mind while simultaneously increasing endurance, strength, and flexibility, elderly people need to prepare and use the right techniques to avoid ending up with sore backs and muscles. Planting a small garden in a raised box is a great alternative if it has become difficult to bend to get down to the ground. If they are determined to get down in the dirt, kneepads will cushion those vital joints. Adaptive garden tools with elongated handles make it much easier to reach the dirt and plants on the ground. Speaking of tools, a wide variety are designed with comfortable grips and spring-action openings geared toward protecting aging joints.

I recommended Antonio purchase a garden kneeler to allow him to sit rather than lean over to reach his tomatoes. This product allows the user to safely assume various positions, including raised kneeling and sitting. When kneeling, it provides soft padding for the knees and promotes use of the arms rather than the back to raise and lower oneself. When turned over it becomes a raised seat.

In thinking about my patients, I can recall several gardening-related incidents that ended in the need for a therapy intervention. One of my patients simply fell over a huge root that had grown up out of the ground. Another gashed her leg when tripping over a metal garden border marker. I will never forget the referral I received that read, "90-year-old man fell out of tree that he was decorating for the holidays. Broke six bones." Cordoning off areas that have roots and objects with sharp, pointed edges in the garden is one good precaution. "Don't climb trees" should go without saying.

Here are some more gardening tips to share with mom and dad:

+ Gardening is exercise, and they should warm up before starting to garden. March in place or take a brisk walk around the block, and stretch their neck, arms, and legs before beginning.

+ Prepare by gathering all of their tools, and determine how best to access the water supply. Hopefully the garden is situated where they can reach it with a lightweight and coiled hose. If it is a distance from the house, link multiple hoses together. Use a hose reel for easy retrieval when done watering.

+ Before beginning, look over all existing equipment such as mowers, ladders, and trimmers to make sure they are still in good working order. Dull blades make work harder, less efficient, and potentially dangerous. Mowers should be tuned up as spring approaches.

+ Read instructions before using lawn chemicals or new gardening equipment.

+ Gardening generally entails the use of mulch, soil, and fertilizer, all of which usually come in heavy bags. Try loading these into a cart or wagon to transport to the garden site, or divide the contents into smaller, more manageable containers.

+ When lifting or pulling out deep weeds, keep their back straight and bend at the knees, lift with the muscles in their legs, and be careful not to twist. When lifting a shovel of dirt, move their feet and turn their whole body rather than twist to the side to dump it.

+ Vary tasks so they do not put too much stress on one part of their body for long periods of time. Change position frequently, and avoid tightly gripping the tools for prolonged periods.

+ Alternate light activities with heavy ones.

+ Plan thirty-minute gardening sessions and spread them out over several days to avoid overexertion. This will also create more work-outs. At the very least, they should take regular rest breaks and stretch the muscles they've been using.

+ Gardening gloves and long pants will help prevent against bug bites, scratches, and poison ivy. To further protect against the elements, it is also a good idea to apply sunscreen and wear a hat and a pair of sunglasses. Wear clothes with pockets to keep a mobile phone close by but not full of schmutz.

+ Keep a water bottle handy, perhaps with ice water, especially if it's hot out.

Snow Shoveling

Often the first snowfall gets us excited and motivated to get out there and clear the driveway, but before grabbing that shovel it is important to be prepared. Share these tips and precautions with mom and dad:

+ Removing heavy, wet snow is a physical activity comparable to lift-ing heavy weights repeatedly and quickly. It involves bending and the use of back, neck, shoulder, trunk, arm, and leg muscles. It also creates strain on the heart. For those who do not regularly exer-cise—and even those who do—the act of shoveling can be a huge strain on the aforementioned muscles.

+ If they have a history of back or heart problems, they should check with their doctor to get clearance for this activity. Dress appropri-ately, including wearing layers of water-repellent clothing that can be adjusted according to the temperature. Be sure to protect hands and face, and wear a hat to keep warmth from escaping. Caution them not to block their vision with scarves so that they can look out for icy patches. On second thought, if they need to wear a scarf over their face, the weather is probably not conducive to being outside shoveling.

+ Having the right equipment is very important. A shovel full of snow may weigh up to 15 pounds. A small shovel will prevent lifting too much snow at one time. The handle should be long enough to keep the back straight when lifting. Look into buying an ergonomically designed shovel that is specifically geared toward injury prevention.

+ Warm up before shoveling, as with any exercise. March in place or complete any aerobic exercise for ten minutes. Add arm and back stretches, and include the large muscle groups of the legs.

+ Separate hands to increase leverage when holding the shovel.

+ Push the snow instead of lifting it.

+ If lifting is necessary, try to keep it to small loads, and make sure to bend the knees and lift with the legs rather than the back. To do this, squat with legs slightly apart, knees bent, and back straight. Lift by straightening the legs without bending at the waist.

+ Walk to where the snow should be dumped and drop it there rather than twisting and throwing it. This will help prevent strain on the spine.

+ Take frequent rest periods. Stand up straight and try some stretches to extend the lower back by placing hands on hips and bending backward slightly for a few seconds. Also stretch arms and legs.

+ Drink plenty of water to stay hydrated.

+ Avoid caffeine and nicotine, as these are stimulants that may increase heart rate, constrict blood vessels, and put strain on the heart.

- If the forecast calls for snow throughout the day, shovel frequently in small intervals rather than letting it pile up.

- Stop and rest if experiencing any pain while shoveling. Resist the temptation to push through the discomfort just to get the job done. Staying safe and healthy is more important.

- Move to Florida.

Raking

If raking leaves is an annual rite of fall where your parents live, remember to add that task to the list of annoying but necessary exterior jobs that requires some adjustments as they get older.

Raking leaves can be a great workout if done correctly. If not, this moderate aerobic physical activity could result in an aching back, shoulders, and wrists. Raking requires twisting, bending, reaching, and lifting, using muscles in the arms, shoulders, chest, legs, and back. As with snow shoveling, good body mechanics will minimize the risk of injury. Look at raking not as an unpleasant chore but as a fall exercise that builds strength in the upper body, core muscles, back, and stomach.

Share the following raking tips with mom and dad:

- Dress in layers before going outside so they can remove clothes to prevent overheating as they get warmer from the exercise.

- Wear sturdy shoes with skid-resistant soles to prevent slipping. Use the right equipment, including an ergonomically designed rake, to help prevent injuries, and wear gloves to protect hands from blisters.

- Before starting, warm up with a brisk walk or marching in place.

- To avoid injury, position legs in a scissor stance (right foot forward, left foot back) and keep reversing leg position at regular intervals throughout the process to avoid excessive strain on one part of the body. Hold the rake handle close to the body and vary the direction in which the rake is pulled (from left to right and then right to left) so that one side of the body is not doing all the work. When raking, try not to twist the spine. Instead, they should move their whole body so that the task is in front of them.

+ Wet leaves are heavier to deal with and also create a slippery work surface. Wait until they dry and are easier to handle. And remember that the leaves may be covering potential hazards such as holes in the ground, rocks, branches, or objects left out on the lawn.

+ Disposing of huge piles of nature's colorful collection generally involves a lot of bending and lifting. If they're filling bags, don't make them too heavy and difficult to transport to the curb for pickup. Good body mechanics means bending the knees and using leg muscles for any lifting. Consider using a wheelbarrow to move the leaves to the curb. If they're dragging a tarp full of leaves, try not to twist the body when pulling it. If possible, have another person grab the opposite corner of the tarp and help with the transport.

+ Rest every ten to twenty minutes.

+ Drink plenty of water to stay hydrated.

+ Rake for a while and switch to another task to avoid stressing the same muscles for an extended period of time. Weather permitting, consider bagging the next day to break up the activities.

+ When finished for the day, cool down with some more stretching activities, and then relax in a warm bath.

Mail and Newspaper Retrieval

As an occupational therapist, I assess my patients' ability to get the mail and newspaper. These two examples of IADLs might seem simple, but they are often difficult for seniors to do. Some are lucky enough to have a mail slot in their front door or a mailbox attached to the house. In more suburban/rural communities, the mailboxes are often found at the end of the driveway. The U.S. Postal Service determines where mailboxes should be placed depending on the location of the house.[1]

If the mailbox is attached to the house, the optimal placement would be a spot where they can grab the mail by opening their front door without having to step outside. If the box is located at the end of their property near the street, make sure their driveway, sidewalks, and, if applicable, roadways are kept clear for mail retrieval. If your parent has balance or mobility issues, a rolling walker with a tray, basket, or seat can be used to walk out to the mailbox and retrieve the mail. It provides support and a place to put the mail when returning to the house. Remind them the mail these days is 99.9 percent bills or junk. What's the rush?

Specifically request that mom or dad's newspaper carrier throw the morning edition onto their front porch. A monetary tip at holiday time may facilitate the desired delivery location. Many seniors are now considering receiving the newspaper only in digital format. In addition to eliminating the need to retrieve the paper out of a snowbank, digital access allows them to enlarge the font to make reading easier. If they're coupon clippers, they can usually opt for a Sunday-only print edition and go with digital the rest of the week. Unfortunately, frequently enjoyed sections such as the crossword puzzle, Jumble, or Sudoku are not fillable online. One remedy is to print out those pages and complete those the old-fashioned way with pen in hand.

Garbage Removal

Many garbage-removal companies have changed over their containers to those that can be rolled out to the curb for pickup. If your parents' company hasn't done so yet, you may just have to ask for the latest containers. Although these can double as a walker on the way out, suggest that mom or dad hang a cane over the handle and use it for balance as they walk back up the driveway after leaving the cart at the curb.

If the bins don't come with wheels, rolling carts may be purchased to transport the garbage receptacles out to where they need to be. Often the containers can stay right in the rolling cart, and the better removal companies will put them back in the cart after emptying the contents. (Again, tips go a long way here.)

With a bit of preplanning, your parents' provider may be willing to allow them to place their receptacles just outside their garage door for pickup instead of all the way down near the street. They will likely have to pay extra for this, but it is worth exploring.

Hacks for Health and Home: The Exterior

+ House numbers should be big, contrast with the exterior color, and be easy to read and locate. Put large reflective house numbers on the mailbox if it is at the end of the driveway, or on a tree or post if the mailbox is not located there. I cannot tell you how many times I have driven around looking for a new patient's house because it was not clearly marked. What if I were an ambulance?

+ Wear sunscreen and protective clothing when working in the garden or, for that matter, when shoveling the snow. They need to protect ears, head, and the back of their neck—areas that are exposed when in the bent-over position.

+ If mom and dad enjoy gardening but do not have space for one, look into joining a community garden. It is also another way to promote socialization.

+ Place decorative garden stakes in dips or unseen holes in the ground to more easily avoid the hazard.

+ Use no-bend weed removers to try to avert back strain from bending down.

+ An automatic garage door opener is a great gadget. I recommend my patients take the opener with them when they go out with others so upon returning they can simply press the button and more easily access the house via the garage. They should always carry a house key as well, on the off chance the power is out or the opener malfunctions.

- Hang a tennis ball on a rope from the ceiling in the garage to help identify the optimal parking position. When the windshield taps the ball, they will know to stop the car. Another option is to mark the wall to coincide with the side mirror so they can stop the car when the mirror matches up with the mark.

- If they are expecting guests, they should keep the garage door opener with them in the house. This way, from the comfort of their recliner, they can press the button and afford access via the garage.

- Solar lights along sidewalks and on deck steps or raised porch steps are great for increasing visibility and safety. This summer I purchased solar garden "flowers" that absorb light from the sun all day and light up my garden all night. These work well to illuminate a walkway.

- If in a cold weather location, keep salt with a scoop or deicer with dispenser close to the door so when they open it they can apply some product before walking onto a slippery surface.

- Great gift for mom or dad . . . If the job of organizing the garage seems too overwhelming, hire a professional organizer to transform the space into a bastion of storage rather than an unsafe collection of junk.

CHAPTER 2

The Entrances and Exits

Selma said: I feel so guilty about my poor children. I am getting weaker every day and can no longer do the stairs. I have so many doctors' appointments and it takes two, sometimes three, people to help me out of this house. I wish I could leave the house for something enjoyable like sitting in the yard or going for a ride or out to lunch but I don't dare ask. I know they would do anything to make me happy, but they have their lives and their kids and their jobs and they can't drop everything to care for their mother.

The daughter said: We are distraught over mom's end-stage cancer diagnosis and the doctor's grim prognosis. The therapy will hopefully help her get a bit stronger, but we also need some ideas on how to help her get out of the house. I am not strong enough to move her alone. My husband is a great help, but he is often out of town on business so I have to wait for my brothers, who live thirty minutes away, to come over. My two young children, while happy that their nana lives with us, are so sad to see her in this condition.

Lynda said: Selma was one of my most challenging patients. She lived with her daughter in an older home built on a sloping lot that required eight steps to access the front door. The family needed several helpers to carry the woman up and down the front stairs. Since it was often difficult to assemble such a group, she was mostly stuck in the house.

In evaluating the home, I noted that the kitchen led out to a large deck that had a long staircase leading down to the backyard. My proposed solution was to think "outside the house!" I suggested we install a stairlift on the back deck staircase. The family was unaware that this was even a possibility. They were now able to wheel her out through the kitchen onto the deck, where she could transfer into the chair and "go for a ride" down to the yard. To protect the stairlift in inclement weather, they covered it with a tarp. She was no longer a prisoner in her own home.

Visitability Getting In and Getting Out

My residential assessments focus on people's ability to safely mobilize in every area of their home. This includes entering and exiting the home itself, a simple function that can be surprisingly difficult. There's mom who can't get up the front steps because there is nothing to hold on to, or dad who doesn't have the endurance to make it from the driveway to the back door. Analyzing every entrance is part of each assessment, and together we formulate an "exit strategy."

Older homes were not built with the concept of "visitability" in mind.[1] Visitability refers to the concept of universal design, where housing is built or renovated in such a way that it can be lived in or visited by anyone with any type of mobility impairment. Let's look at some of the essential features of visitability with regards to entrances and exits in our parents' homes.

Getting to the Front Door

Entranceways to homes are as diverse as the homes themselves. The ideal scenario is to have a no-step entrance to the house, also referred to as a zero threshold. This can be accomplished by grading the walkway from the driveway and/or front sidewalk to lead up to the front door via a slow, gradual pitch. In essence, you are creating a ramp out of the sidewalk. Most landscapers should know how to do this. The picture on the next page is an attractive way to accomplish a no-step entrance by using planting areas to border the "ramp." The sidewalk should end in a 5-foot-square flat landing that provides plenty of room for a wheelchair to turn.

Front entrances without a zero threshold usually have some type of stairway leading to either a porch or a platform that brings you to the front door. To work toward overcoming obstacles, it is important to

first understand the composition of the stairway. The parts of a step include the tread, which is the horizontal part that your foot steps on, and the riser, which is the vertical measurement of each stair. Closed risers have a vertical surface between the steps that your toe touches. Open risers, often seen on outdoor decks or winding staircases, have open space between treads. The height of risers and treads should meet local municipal building codes. Older homes are often not up to the latest construction regulations. To give you an idea of what to look for to assess the safety of your parents' entranceways, outside risers should measure between a minimum of 4 inches and a maximum of 7½ inches high. The ideal width of the tread is 11 inches.

When evaluating the staircase, first look at the condition of the steps. They should be repaired or replaced if they are cracked or crumbling. If the riser is too high, it may have become too hard for mom and dad to "climb" the stairs. If the rise is inconsistent, balance can easily be thrown off. That being said, most of the time there is not a lot we can do with the stairs themselves, but the following adaptations can make getting up and down easier and safer.

Railings

Railings are a must. The ideal situation is to have one on both sides of the stairs so mom or dad can hold on with both hands as they go up and down. If the stairway is wide and they are unable to hold both railings at the same time, the presence of two railings will allow them to use their dominant side in either direction. The two pictures to the right illustrate a modification I recommended to remedy a staircase where the railings were particularly far apart. We had a railing installed down the middle

of the staircase to facilitate the ability to hold on to both sides. The photos at the bottom of the page show a clever invention that a patient's husband built. He made a wooden rail that slides out when his wife is

going to use the stairs and then back between the slots of the existing iron railing when not needed.

Another common situation I encounter is that railings do not extend beyond the top and bottom steps. If at all possible, railings should be extended to give needed support to steady oneself before stepping on or off the staircase.

It seems that frequently the final step leading into an older house is very high. An easy fix is to create a platform of some type to reduce the rise of this last step. The picture below illustrates a homemade step that a patient's son built out of decking material.

A product called an outdoor step is an inexpensive and safe way to reduce the rise in half when stepping in or out of the house. It is a sturdy platform with a rubber surface to prevent slippage. It is lightweight and works well with any high step, whether outdoors or indoors. Search "outdoor step" online to learn more about these handy products.

Ramps

If stairs have become a hardship to negotiate, there are many types of ramps that can facilitate getting in and out of the house, especially for seniors who require the use of a wheelchair. For those who use a walker or cane, great care needs to be taken to prevent falls on this sloping surface. Those wearing bifocals may also have difficulty judging the slope and distance of the ramp.

Ramps are most often made out of wood, steel, or aluminum and are available in various heights and widths. Regardless of which material is chosen, it is very important to have a nonslip surface to promote safe usage. To figure out the length of the ramp sufficient to cover your space, measure the height of the steps you are ramping. Americans with Disabilities Act (ADA) guidelines call for a slope of 12 inches for every 1 inch of rise. So, if the rise of the steps is 18 inches from the pavement to the threshold of the front door, you would need a ramp that is 216 inches (18 feet long). The 1:12 slope-to-raise ratio is fairly steep, and people who self-propel their own wheelchairs may have difficulty negotiating this incline if they do not have good upper-body strength. If space allows, a ratio of 1:20, which calculates to a 30-foot-long ramp in our scenario, would make it much easier to navigate.[2]

Landings are necessary at the top and bottom of the ramp and at intermediate levels to provide areas to rest and to accommodate for turning if the ramp changes direction. The landings should be 5 feet long to provide enough space for a wheelchair to make a full turn. Ramps should also have handrails on both sides and a 3- to 4-inch bottom guardrail the length of both sides of the ramp to act as a curb, preventing a wheelchair or walker from slipping off the surface.

There are beautiful wooden ramps, usually permanent ones, that can blend in with the landscaping and enhance the entranceway to the home. The one depicted above is the front of a New England beach house. Modular aluminum ramps are available for purchase or rent and are available in various lengths and widths. They can be used for the front entranceway or those few steps from the garage into the house. Folding or "suitcase" ramps are lightweight and portable and can be easily transported for use in various locations.

Stairlifts

Another remedy for getting in and out of the house is to install an electric stairlift. As Selma's family discovered, these are not only available for the inside of a house. Outdoor models need to be protected against inclement weather, generally by covering them with a tarp. If fallen leaves and snow are part of your normal weather pattern, you'll need to clean the stairlift track periodically to ensure proper operation.

The picture above left illustrates a starilift that enabled one of my patients to get into her split-level home. She also has two additional lifts installed in the interior, thereby allowing her access to all levels of the house. Above right illustrates a 92 -year-old who lives in her beach house in North Carolina. She is determined to successfully age in place!

Vertical platform lifts are elevators that raise a person from the ground level up to the entry level of a house. They can be used even if the person is in a wheelchair or standing with the assistance of a walker. Consider installing one when there is no room for a regular ramp or when the goal is to reach a higher place like the second floor. Unfortunately they are fairly expensive, making them not practical for everyone.

Finally—Getting Through the Front Door

I want you to go outside on your front step or porch right now and take a look at your welcome mat. Has the design on it long since faded? Does it have a few holes in it from the countless shoes that have stepped on it through the years? Does it slip when you try to move it by pushing it with your foot? If so, join the club . . . and then go out and treat yourself to a new one!

Now, go do the same thing at your parents' house. (You think your mat is bad? Theirs has probably been there since 1972!) The replacement mat should be large and heavy so it doesn't move when someone rubs their shoes or boots on it to clean off the debris. That said, make sure it is not so thick as to cause a tripping hazard.

A light fixture installed on the front porch or over the front door is essential for providing illumination, especially when fumbling for the keys or when inside and attempting to identify a visitor. Having exterior lights on timers ensures the periphery of the property is always well lit and precludes the need to remember to turn on lights. Motion-sensor lights are particularly helpful near the driveway, at entrances to the house, and focused on the backyard. They light the way and also serve as a deterrent for unwanted guests. A lighted doorbell makes it easy to find the keyhole and provides extra illumination if the porch light goes out.

One interesting universal design recommendation is to install a shelf next to the front door to hold packages or purses so hands can be free for opening the door. My personal solution was to place an antique wicker bench next to my front door that serves this purpose. I like the bench idea, as it also doubles as a place to sit to adjust boots, wait for a ride, or watch people go by.

The ideal width for the front door is 36 inches, which provides 32 inches of clearance to accommodate a wheelchair. A good safety feature is to install a window on at least one side of the door frame to allow for viewing visitors. For added security, opt for tempered, laminated, or some other type of reinforced glass that's more difficult to break. Peepholes are another option, as long as they are the right height for mom or dad to use.

The ideal external threshold is no more than 1/2 inch high. Any higher can be a hazard for anyone with mobility issues or for those who need a wheelchair. If the threshold is too high, a carpenter can bevel or smooth it out. Another option is a portable threshold ramp, usually made of aluminum or rubber. These also work great for the threshold where a sliding glass door leads out to the back of the house. The one pictured above is a homemade wooden ramp. For more information and to see pictures of these handy items, search "portable threshold ramps."

Door Handles

Lever door handles are the easiest to use for anyone with weakness or decreased mobility and coordination in their hands. They can be maneuvered with a closed fist or even an elbow if hands are full. Even my dog can jump up and open the lever handle on my bathroom door! When people look at me incredulously when I tell them that, I direct them to the video of her exploits on my website, otherwisehealthy.com.[3]

Attached Garages

Often the second entrance/egress to the house is through the garage. If there are a couple of steps from the garage into the house, install a railing to improve access and safety. If possible, extend the railing beyond the stairs, and install it 1½ inches away from the wall. This will provide sufficient room for good gripping while making it tight enough to prevent an arm from getting caught between the wall and the rail. Another easy fix to help getting in or out of the house is to install a safety handle or grab bar on either side of the doorway, either in an existing wall or in the doorjamb.

A new "over 55" condo development in my neighborhood did a great job with the transition from the garages into the units. Instead of tall, skinny steps, they built one large platform, wide enough for a walker to be placed on it, between the garage floor and the inside of the condo. They also placed a railing on the wall. This modification can be easily done in most garages. It reduces the number of steps to two and allows for a safe platform to step on if the user is dependent on a walker.

It goes without saying that the path from the door to the car or outside to the driveway should be kept clear. Place garbage and recycling bins near enough to the door so they can easily be accessed during the week.

Declutter and Organize the Garage

Years of accumulated stuff can begin to encroach on the safe and easy access to your parents' garage. Organizing the garage is an undertaking that should not be tackled alone, and sharing it with mom or dad can be a catalyst for discussing future issues that will be arising (such as when to give up the keys to the car and when to hire someone else to maintain the grounds). Save this project for a warm, dry stretch of at least two days in a row. That said, don't wait forever. You enhance safety *and* relieve stress when the car can easily be driven into the garage. With attached garages, the goal is for easy access into the house via an unobstructed path.

Before beginning, formulate a plan for how to remove unwanted items. This may include leftover chemicals, paints, cleaning supplies, and other hazardous materials, not to mention old bicycles, broken lawnmowers, rakes with two tines left—you get the picture. Know what can be put out in the trash, what may need to go to a public dumpster or hauled to the dump, and what would be considered hazardous waste that has to be disposed of properly. The town clerk or city hall should have that information.

The first step is to take everything out of the garage and place it out on the driveway (hence the need for the weather check) to easily inventory everything that has been lurking in the recesses for years. Once emptied, it is a good time to sweep the garage floor and clean the walls and floors.

Next is the initial purge. Throw everything away that snuck in there and hasn't been touched in years. Get rid of the greasy, dirty, rusty, broken items whose purpose has been forgotten. Your parents will enjoy seeing the progress as the trash pile grows and more free space instantly becomes available. Once the real garbage is gone, hone down the rest into four piles: (1) keep, (2) give away or donate, (3) sell, and (4) throw away. When we get inside the house in the next few chapters, there will much more detail on decluttering and getting rid of stuff. For our garage project, these four piles will suffice.

Start categorizing the items that have made it into the "keep" pile. Common categories include garbage and recycling bins, garden supplies, useable paint, bug sprays and other chemical products, tools, recreational gear, automotive items, lawn care equipment, seasonal decorations, and anything else that is deemed worthy of living in the garage. The purpose for this step is to make it easier to begin the next one: storing related items together for easy retrieval.

At this point, start planning where everything should go when it's put back in the garage. One approach is to first map out the placement of everything on a piece of paper, so before putting things back your folks can think about when and how often each item is used. If, for example, mom saves a box of toys for the grandchildren when they visit from across the country twice a year, or if dad has a box of Christmas decorations, those can go on a top shelf, clearly labeled and out of the way. On the other hand, the garbage and recycling bins should probably be placed near the door leading into the house so they can be easily accessed on a regular basis.

Things that are frequently used should end up on a shelf that is between waist and eye level. This will preserve joints and lessen chances of an injury when reaching for an item. Again, lesser-used items should more appropriately be stored on either a high or low shelf, essentially not taking up space that's needed for daily garage use. That said, if you're worried about mom or dad using ladders or step stools to reach items on high shelves, don't store things too high.

Once it has been decided what to keep and how much space will be designated to each category of items, go out and purchase appropriate storage products. Wall-mounted pegboards and wire grids are great for vertically storing grab-and-go things like lawn and garden tools and recreational gear. Shelving can be freestanding or built-in, and containers are available in many different shapes and sizes. My preference is covered tubs made of clear plastic to more easily identify the contents and small jars for storing things like loose nails, screws, and other small bits of hardware. I use trash cans to store my collection of garden stakes, but this type of container is also great as an alternative to wall hooks for brooms, rakes, and anything else that needs to be stored upright.

The final step is to put everything back in its new home. This is the fun part, as now there is a place for everything and everything will be in its place. (Full disclosure: I may not have originated that phrase.)

Hacks for Health and Home: Entrances and Exits

+ Having a covered entranceway is so nice when you are fumbling for the keys and it is raining. If this is not part of the original house, a roof extension or awning can be added.

+ If there is a ramp made of wood, apply paint mixed with one pound of silica sand per gallon of paint to create traction.

+ Be sure to have large, reflective house numbers located in an easy-to-spot site somewhere on the front of the house and at the end of the driveway. This will aid emergency personnel needing to find the house, not to mention it will be more convenient for home therapists like me.

+ Research "ergonomic key turners," which are curved handles that provide extra leverage to turn a key in the lock. These are great for those with weakness or decreased mobility and range of motion in their hands and wrists.

CHAPTER 3

The Living Room, Dining Room, and General Living Areas

Donald said: I took this old chair from my law office when I retired. Believe it or not it was in my father's law office before that. The leather has held up all these years, and it is the softest, most comfortable chair I have ever sat in. Every night I sit in it to read the paper and watch the news. Joan and the kids say they would like to get me a new one for my birthday, but I don't want a new chair. It brings back a lifetime of great memories. Besides, there is nothing wrong with this chair.

Joan said: We have to figure out what to do about the chair my husband sits on in the den. When he is about 10 feet away from the chair, he parks his walker way in the corner, careens around the coffee table, and unsteadily walks over to it and plops right down. It's a wonder he hasn't cracked a vertebra with the way he drops into the chair. What's worse is he cannot get up on his own. He always needs me to loop my arm under his and give him a boost up. This is getting more difficult as I deal with my extremely sore shoulder. He will deny there are any problems, but at some point one of us is going to get hurt.

Lynda says: In assessing Donald, I observed how he transferred both on and off of his favorite chair. There was no question that he had difficulty in both directions. The chair—a classic that clearly held many wonderful years of fond memories—currently represented an obstacle for both him and his wife.

The first step was to create more navigable room around the chair by repositioning it back away from the coffee table. This also allowed

Donald to park his walker much closer to the chair, eliminating the dangerous distance from where he was leaving it. I then had Joan purchase chair risers at the local home goods store to raise the height of the chair 4 inches. My treatment plan included teaching Donald strengthening exercises for his arms and legs and the safe and effective method to transfer on and off a chair. In no time he could independently get on and off with ease, saving his back, her shoulder, and the chair.

The Furniture

When thinking about safety and mobility throughout the living areas in a house, we often neglect to take a close look at the furniture to assess its user-friendliness. The furniture, you ask? Mom and dad's living room has had the same large velvet upholstered camel-back couch, satin-striped side chairs, and the desk with the claw feet since we first landed a man on the moon. Dad would not consider giving up his favorite chair in the den, even though the cushions are so worn they provide no support. Mom's piano has been in the same spot in the living room since they got married, and she considers it her pride and joy.

Assessing how our parents are doing is an ongoing fact-finding mission. For furniture, we need to observe if they have trouble getting on and off specific pieces (or all of it). Do they "plop" down into their chair? Do they need three tries and some extra heavy breathing before they can get off the couch? Take a look at the chairs and couches and assess the height, the firmness of the seat, and the type of arms, if any. Arthritic knees and hips, general weakness acquired if they didn't keep up an exercise regime, and/or the countless number of physical diagnoses that can decrease mobility can wreak havoc on the ability to get on and off of a low, forty-year-old cushion.

If this describes your folks, don't despair. There are easy modifications that can be done to existing furniture. The rule of thumb is the higher the height of a chair or couch, the easier it is to get on and off. Let's see how we can accomplish that.

Risers

An easy fix for low-standing furniture is to purchase furniture risers. They can be found in most home goods stores, plus places like Target, Bed Bath & Beyond, and Staples. The risers are blocks of various shapes and sizes, made of rubber or wood, and with heights of 3½ to 7 inches (bed risers are usually higher; 3 to 4 inches is all you need for chairs and couches). They only work if there are legs or feet on the bottom of the chair or couch in question. The riser should have a cavity in which the foot of the furniture rests to ensure it doesn't slip off.

If the chair or couch does not have legs—for example a rocking chair or glider—the risers won't work. One way to remedy this is to build a 3- to 4-inch-high platform to place under the entire chair. Be sure there is a lip around the edges so the chair won't slip off. This is where the handy person in the family comes into play.

Another option is to build up height by placing a firm cushion on top of the existing one. If a couch has several cushions, consider pulling the middle cushion out and placing it on top of the one near an arm. You could also use a throw pillow or cushion from another chair for this same purpose. Take care that the additional cushion is pushed against the back of the couch and sturdy enough so it doesn't slip off. Folding up a blanket and putting it under the existing cushion is another remedy that works well. This will add needed height and be virtually invisible as the cushion settles down on top of it.

Firm seats are helpful in easing transfers on and off of furniture. Consider switching the cushions around on a couch if there is one that has been less used and has maintained its shape and support. You can also consider buying a new piece of foam, cutting it to fit, and making a new cushion.

The higher the back on a chair the better the back support, and it's very helpful to have at least one arm to help push off and let oneself down without the aforementioned plop. This is why I always recommend that my patients sit to one side of a couch within reach of an arm and never in the middle.

Seat Lifts and Couch Canes

If mom or dad are still unable to get up with the modifications discussed above, consider a seat lift. Seat lifts are cushions that are placed on the existing chair or couch cushion and gently lift the person out of the chair and lower them back in. They are operated manually with a pneumatic pump or are electrically powered. It's an inexpensive solution and viable alternative to a full lift chair (more on these in the following pages). Research "seat lift" for more information.

Couch canes are handy products that aid users when they transition from standing to sitting and back up again from a chair, couch, or recliner. Place the base under the couch or chair so it doesn't slip during use. The wide adjustable height handle will provide a stable fixture to hold on to. Research "couch cane" for more on these lift chair alternatives.

Lift Chairs

Lift chairs have proven to be a godsend to many with whom I have worked. These motorized chairs, operated via a handheld remote control, lift the user to an almost standing position and recline in the opposite direction to an almost fully reclined position. They are upholstered in materials ranging from leather to vinyl to cloth and come in sizes from petite to bariatric.

If you are considering one of these for your parents, I highly recommend contacting a reputable home medical supply company that knows how to determine the correct size, type, and options in your price range. The one feature I insist my patients look for is a chair with no space between the seat and footrest when the chair is in the reclining position. Such a space does not provide continuous support, which can cause pressure areas on the back of the legs, and it could create a hazard if their legs get caught in the gap.

Lift chairs are especially good for people who have chronic obstructive pulmonary disease (COPD) and other breathing difficulties. The chair enables them to rest while keeping their head elevated, which in turn eases breathing. I find that many of my patients end up sleeping in their lift chairs rather than their bed. At first the kids worry about this, but they come to understand it better once they see that it is often the best way for mom and dad to rest comfortably and easily get in and out of "bed."

Another option when considering a lift chair is a Risedale chair. Only the seat cushion elevates, and the style of chair is a classic open-legged wing back so it often fits in easily with the décor. It takes up less room then a classic lift chair, and if the user only needs a boost up it is a great option. Search "Risedale chair" for more information.

If you believe your parent is sleeping full-time in a lift chair, explore with them their reasons for doing so. If they admit they do so because they are having problems getting in and out of bed but desire to return to bed, there are remedial steps that can be attempted (which we'll discuss in chapter 5). If they desire to sleep in the chair because it eases their breathing and the mechanical benefits offer added comfort and less strain on their joints, then what they have chosen may be a good solution. The caveat: be sure they don't develop any pressure areas on their back or buttocks from sitting and lying in only one position. You can't turn on your side when sleeping in a lift chair. I tell my patients to get up and walk every two to three hours, and lay on their sides on their "real" beds for a rest each day if possible.

Furniture Placement

With many seniors, the location of their furniture has remained static since it was first delivered, and they rarely consider making what are often simple tweaks to enhance the livability of the space. At this stage, furniture should be arranged to create clear pathways and good accessibility. One thing I often encounter in a client's home is a large item, like a desk or piano, placed against a wall close to the opening of the next room. This placement generally results in having to walk around it every time they go in and out of the room. By simply sliding this piece of furniture a foot or so down the wall away from the doorway, entering and exiting becomes much easier.

Another scenario that often leads to trouble is when the coffee table is placed too close to the couch. If mom or dad uses a walker, watch to see what they do with it when they get near the couch. More than likely they "park" the walker right before the coffee table and slip in between the couch and table while holding on to nothing. One remedy would be to move the coffee table out a few extra inches, creating ample room to hold on to their walker and use it for support as they approach the couch and turn around and sit.

Furniture Walking

Let's talk about a little phenomenon that therapists see all the time: furniture walking. Picture mom and dad as they get up from one spot and grab various pieces of furniture for support as they meander to their intended destination. First they grab the back of the chair to get their balance, walk a few steps, and then pause again as they hold on to the desk situated against the wall. They leave the desk and teeter in space for a solid 8 feet until they can "touch down" by holding the back of the couch. Then with one last thrust they push off, glide along the wall, and finally head into the bathroom.

Furniture walking can be problematic if they are cruising through large, open areas with nothing to hold on to or if they have balance issues. Although the use of a walker would be beneficial, I find either no one has recommended it, they have refused to use one, or it doesn't easily fit through their cluttered pathways. If you're facing that last situation, take a fresh look at the areas around large pieces of furniture and the walking pathways in each room and see if it's possible to create large-enough spaces for a walker, generally 36 inches in width, to comfortably fit through. Then have a discussion about the benefits of using a walker.

If they have been furniture walking for a long time and the space is tight enough so they can easily go from landing to landing, it might actually be a workable situation. There are times when I will evaluate a situation and determine that furniture walking is acceptable and safe. In the bathroom, many have to park their walker outside and hold on to countertops to make their way to the toilet or shower. When trying to complete a task in the kitchen, it can be a real pain to drag the walker. If the counter configuration and table placement are good, they can often safely hold on to those surfaces and get around the kitchen without difficulty. The other place is the bedroom. If the bed and dresser are really close, they can park the walker near the foot of the bed and use the dresser to guide them to the head of the bed, where they can sit down.

Other Living Area Considerations

There's more to the general living areas than just the furniture. Things like lights, walking surfaces, phones, and windows should be evaluated for safety and convenience.

Lighting and Electrical

Electrical and phone cords should always be secured and not obstructing any pathways. Run them along the wall if possible and not under rugs or furniture, where they can't be monitored and could get frayed or damaged, causing a fire hazard.

Light switches should ideally be placed in an accessible location near the entrance to a room. If you research the best height to mount switches, you may come up with several different answers. General guidelines call for light switches and other environmental controls to be mounted between 42 and 48 inches from the finished floor to the center of the switch. Illuminated touch or rocker-type switches are the easiest to use. Regular lamps can be easily converted to touch-sensitive lamps, which are activated by the touch of a hand rather than by a switch.

Good lighting is a key safety feature of any home, and as we age we need more light. Be sure mom and dad are using the correct wattage bulbs in their old lamps. It is unsafe to exceed maximum recommended wattages, especially in old fixtures. On the other hand, it is unwise to keep lights too dim in an effort to save on the electric bill. Eye fatigue occurs faster as we age, and we can see things easier by enhancing our lighting. Unfortunately, since eyesight varies from person to person, there is no one magic light bulb that works for everyone.

What does work for older people is to reduce glare and use task lighting in areas that are in high use, such as near the chair where mom sits to read the paper or at the desk where dad pays his bills. Having a lamp or torchiere that can be directed, such as on a moveable stem, is very helpful, as it can provide upward lighting for general illumination or spot lighting for various tasks. You can find inexpensive torchiere lamps at places like Target. Other high-need areas for focused lighting are the kitchen, bathroom, sewing room, and dining areas.

Floor Surfaces

The ideal flooring is one that is flat with no changes in surface at all. As mom and dad age, both their vision and balance are likely to get worse.

You need to consider how this natural deterioration is impacted by the changes in surfaces as they walk around the house.

If carpeting is preferred, one with a low pile of less than 1/2 inch is optimal. This means the shag rug that has adorned the living room for years must go. (My guess is that it's green or gold, right?) Wood, linoleum, and tile are easier for wheelchair users. These surfaces should be kept clean (dust and pet hair can cause slipping) but not so highly polished that they become slippery. If opting for tile, select a type with texture for more traction.

Throw Rugs

Let's have a little chat about throw rugs—the bane of the therapist's existence. Throw or scatter rugs have been around since prehistoric times, when animal skins were placed at the cave door to keep predators away. The ones in mom's house have probably been there nearly as long.

To decide if we can let mom keep her rugs, the first thing to assess is the condition of their underside. Chances are that the backing on old rugs has worn down, making them slippery. Try the "Shrager twist test" to determine if the rug is safe. Simply step on the rug with your

feet about 12 inches apart, wiggle your hips, and try to do the twist. Music is optional. If the rug moves under your feet, it is not safe.

The next consideration is the size of the rug. Large area rugs and long hall runners generally do not provide a hazard as long as they are not frayed and are wide enough so they don't move. The patient's home shown in the photo below had a collection of huge oriental rugs that did not slip or slide. I deemed them safe. Move your focus to the smaller slippery rugs that often need replacing. Many of my patients have attempted to solve the slippery rug problem by putting rubber mats under them or trying to secure them in place with tape. My experience is that these solutions are often less than satisfactory, as the rug tends to get displaced from the rubber backing or the tape loses its adhesiveness and becomes a hazard in itself.

If they have a deep affection for a few small rugs, perhaps a compromise is to place them in a low-traffic area such as under a side table or in the corner of the dining room under a pretty plant stand or floor lamp. This way they get to keep the rug and you get to not be up all night worrying.

Telephones

Many of the older homes I visit still have an outdated corded wall phone that is not optimally located, probably still hanging in the kitchen where it was first installed. I always recommend the use of portable or cordless phones with a base in the bedroom next to the bed and additional handsets located in the kitchen, the den, and/or the living room. With many portable phones nowadays, only the base of the main phone needs to be plugged into both power and a phone jack, while the additional handsets can be stored in charging bases that simply need to be plugged into an electrical outlet. Such systems make for optimal placement, as there are several outlets around the house that can be used. If the cordless phones charge all night, they are fine to be off their base all day and should be carried around by mom so there is always a phone within reach. I remind my patients to take a handset with them when going to the bathroom, down to the basement, or out to the garage where falls may occur and they might otherwise not be able to call for help.

Of course a cellular phone will provide the same benefits and is even smaller and thus easier to transport. There are countless types of phones on the market designed with the elderly in mind. Look for ones that have large, lighted numbers and a feature where the sound can be amplified if needed.

Windows

There are many different types of windows, depending on the architecture of a house. The more windows, the more natural light is available to illuminate life inside. Over time, access to the windows may become partially blocked due to accumulated furniture and other objects. From a safety and operational standpoint, make sure to clear the clutter to create sufficient access to your parents' windows. Whatever the window type, it is important to check that they easily open and close, have hardware that is easily operated by mom or dad, and that the locks are in secure working order. If access to window treatments is a problem, one remedy is to install drapes and blinds that are remotely controlled.

Declutter and Organize the Living Areas

If all our parents had was furniture in their houses, there would be little clutter . . . but the environment would be quite boring. No color, no texture, no sensory stimulation. No pillows on the couches, no artwork on the walls, no family photos gracing the end tables, no decorative bowls from the islands or flower-filled vases on the coffee table, and no collection of grandma's china in the wall unit.

Being surrounded by things gathered over the years makes us happy, evokes wonderful memories, and defines our sense of self. The problem arises when we start running out of room and can no longer maintain it all. A pretty wicker basket on the kitchen table becomes a receptacle spilling over with mail, the pile of magazines in the bathroom is stacked halfway up the wall, and the collection of snow globes gathered from vacations is covered with dust. Clutter in itself causes a buildup of excess dust, which may exacerbate breathing disorders such as asthma, and makes it harder to get around safely.

There is no time like the present to take a fresh look at your parents' home, because cherished belongings accumulated over a lifetime morph into clutter so slowly that it is often not noticed. An interesting exercise is for both you and them to do a walk-though and role-play that you are guests for the very first time in the house. Take note of everything that seems cluttered, dirty, or dingy or is hindering mobility around the house.

You may find that what once was a neat and uncluttered house has transformed into various sections of overflowing stuff, with things that your parents need most "buried under the rubble." The simultaneous feeling of knowing they need to get the clutter under control but being overwhelmed and not knowing where to begin sets up a constant feeling of stress. Too much stress can contribute to myriad health problems.

Where to begin? One approach I like to get the ball rolling is an "initial blitz purge." Start by evaluating the real junk, the stuff that has absolutely no real value—sentimental or monetary—but has somehow quietly accumulated over the years to the point where they have become blind to its existence. Look around the living room, den, and dining room with a critical eye and a goal to throw away as much stuff as you can. The pile of old magazines and newspapers next to the couch, the pens that don't write that are on or in the desk, the half-chewed dog bones and the grandkid's broken toy parts that rolled under the chair—all of it should be thrown away. Let's not forget the bowl of beaded plastic fruit on the dining room table or the dried flowers in the vase that have more dust than leaves. You might have to make more than one pass through each room to be sure you catch it all.

When that is done, the serious decluttering begins. It is best to break this daunting job into bite-sized pieces. Plan to work on one room or one cabinet or closet at a time. Creating a time limit often helps to make this project more manageable. For example, "We will focus on the big closet in the den for two hours and then take a break. Our goal will be to only work on the closet today." Stick to your time limit, avoid distractions, and schedule a time when you can return to that same area and continue the project. If you first tackle a room that they frequently use, the noticeable results will create positive reinforcement and increase the drive to keep the decluttering going. Be respectful and thoughtful, and remember that this is their stuff you're clearing out, and you are working together.

Categorize items into five groups: (1) keep, (2) give away, (3) sell or garage sale potential, (4) charitable donations, and of course, (5) the all-important throw-away pile. Notice I didn't list a "maybe" pile. Let me share the OHIO rule with you. This stands for "Only Handle It Once," meaning no "hold till later" to make a decision. Each item can only go into one of these five groups. The exception to this rule would be important papers, because you don't want to waste a lot of time reading through every document now. Place them in a big box that your folks can look through at their leisure.

How do they decide what to keep and what goes to one of the other piles? Start by having them define what use the item has in their life. If they haven't used it in over a year, they could probably live without it. Is it beautiful and do they love it, or are they just keeping it out of habit? Are they saving it hoping their children or grandchildren will want it? Examine the nature of their attachment to an object, as often it is the meaning behind the item and not the item itself that makes it hard to part with. Was it given to them by a special person, or does it depict a very special occasion in their life? Ultimately they need to determine the worst that could happen if the item gets thrown out, and whether their life will be negatively impacted if it is no longer in their possession.

Share these additional organizing tips with mom and dad:

+ Use the in-out rule. For every item that comes into their home (new books, videos, clothes, toys, etc.), another comparable item should go out.

+ Stay ahead of clutter. Sort and file mail daily. Keep newspapers until the next edition arrives. Clip and file specific articles they want to keep and then discard the magazine.

+ Organize items in clear plastic storage boxes with lids. This reduces dust and makes it easy to identify what is inside. Small objects can be kept in ziplock bags or plastic boxes with compartments.

+ Photograph or videotape cherished items they have decided to part with. That way they save the memory and let go of the object.

+ If items they are throwing out are too big and heavy to handle, consider a professional junk remover such as 1-800-Got-Junk or College Hunks Hauling Junk. (I might have something removed just to check them out.)

Hacks for Health and Home: Living Areas of the Home

+ Be sure mom knows how to use the remote control on her lift chair properly. The leg rest must be down and under the front of the chair before she gets up. I often find my patients do not "close" the chair properly, creating a tripping hazard when they go to stand up.

+ Never "run" to answer the phone, as many falls occur this way. Set up an answering machine so there's no need to worry about a missed call.

+ Use the pocket of a walker bag or wear an apron with pockets to transport small items like the phone around the house.

+ When choosing lighting fixtures, purchase those that take a three-way bulb so they can increase the lighting using a single switch.

+ Make sure mom and dad's shoes have good tread on the bottoms, as regardless of the type of flooring, footwear may contribute to falls.

+ Get mom and dad into the habit of double-checking that after concluding a conversation, they have properly hung up or turned off the phone. A visual prompt may do the trick, such as a sign on the hook or charger where the phone is kept that says "Hang up or turn off the phone" accompanied by an adorable picture of their grandchild holding a phone. It can be quite frustrating to hear a constant busy signal over an extended time frame when you want to make sure they are okay. We often called my father-in-law on his cell phone to tell him to hang up the house phone.

+ Use feather dusters for light cleaning. They weigh next to nothing and provide less strain to hands.

+ Vacuuming can put a lot of strain on the spine and neck. Keep the hose in front of the body at waist height, use both hands to push the vacuum, and walk straight across the carpet. Then turn and go back. Avoid pushing and pulling in short little strokes.

+ A central vacuum system reduces the need to haul around the vacuum cleaner, eliminates the need to empty/change vacuum bags, and removes the hazard associated with electrical cords in your pathway.

CHAPTER 4

The Kitchen

Eunice said: I lived in this apartment with my sister for eight years until she died two months ago. Now all I have is my cat Annabelle who is 16 years old. I could not stay here independently without "my girls" who care for me so well. The other day, Annabelle was meowing so loudly I thought something had happened to her. My aide had gone down to get my mail and grab milk from the little store in the lobby. I got out of my lift chair very slowly and walked with my walker from the bedroom to the kitchen. There was Annabelle sitting in front of her empty bowl, howling and looking so upset. The cans of cat food were in the pantry on a shelf I couldn't reach, so I pulled out a little stool to use just this once. I climbed up on the first step, being careful to hold on to the counter, and next thing I knew I was on the floor. I guess I lost my balance. I could not move and my hip was in terrible pain. Thankfully my aide returned right after that.

The aide said: I was gone from the apartment for ten minutes! When I left, Eunice was dozing in her lift chair. When I came back, the cat was meowing wildly. I ran into the kitchen and there was Eunice, lying on her side. The stool, normally safely tucked under the pantry shelf, was pulled out and a can of cat food was on the floor. I called the paramedics.

Lynda said: Eunice has private aides twenty-four hours a day who only leave briefly to run errands. She decided she could reach the cat food by climbing onto an old stool with four little rickety feet and a worn surface. She lost her balance, fell back onto her side, and fractured her left hip. In my more than thirty-seven years of treating the senior population, I have found that most falls in the kitchen are a result of someone trying to reach up into a cabinet or shelf.

The key to making our living spaces safer as we age involves making logical and often simple adaptations to existing conditions. In Eunice's case, I had her put the cat food on a lower shelf so she wouldn't have to climb to reach it. And I convinced her to replace that crummy old stool with a modern, safer model!

The General Space

The kitchen is often the heart of the home, the place where family and friends tend to congregate. It is here where holiday meals and generations of beloved recipes are prepared. Many of us can conjure up the aromas that would greet us from the kitchen as we opened the front door, from chicken soup to spaghetti sauce to freshly baked chocolate chip cookies.

Although a large renovation to alter the size and overall layout of the kitchen may be prohibitive, there are ways to modify areas to make it a safer place to negotiate.

When I do an assessment of the kitchen, I look at the type of appliances, the height of the countertops, the accessibility of the cabinets, the positioning of the table, and the overall space for mobility within the room.

In general, an open floor plan makes it easier for two people to be in the kitchen together, and if one is on crutches or using a walker, the wider the open space the more room to move around. If one of your parents is in a wheelchair, a 5-foot diameter of open space is an ideal turning radius for them. That said, I have a special place in my heart for galley-type kitchens, which usually have a narrow passageway between two parallel walls with counters that can be held on to as a person walks down the middle.

Flooring

Easy-to-maintain, slip-resistant flooring is the best option for safety in the kitchen. If the floor is old, it is likely not made of slip-resistant material. Tile or marble can be very slippery, especially when wet.

Suggest to mom that she consider applying anti-slip products to the floor (research "anti-slip floor treatments"), avoid floor wax, and be careful when using cleaners. I sprayed my stainless refrigerator with a cleaner and some apparently landed on the floor, creating an ice-skating rink in front of the fridge!

Countertops

If one were following universal design guidelines, it would be ideal to have varying heights of countertops to accommodate people of any height and those who need to be seated when working. The most comfortable and controllable working height for the hands is that which places the wrists slightly below the elbows. Since the elbow of the average-height person is slightly higher than 36 inches above the floor, a kitchen counter height of 34 to 36 inches is appropriate for someone standing.

It is best to have at least 18 to 24 inches of cleared countertop space on at least one side of the oven, cooktop, microwave, and sink on which hot or heavy items can be placed to "rest" for a moment. This allows mom or dad to get their balance and get a good grip on the item with both hands before moving it to its destination. The countertops near the oven and cooktop should be heat resistant for easy and safe transfer of hot dishes.

Unless a large renovation is possible, changing the height of the counters is probably not an option. Alternatively, the kitchen table can be used as a workstation, or a portable kitchen island can be added to the space. These are great, as they are on wheels for easy mobility, come in all sorts of sizes and heights, and have options such as pullout drawers, open cabinets underneath for additional storage, spice caddies, and knife holders. Be sure the caster wheels have easy locking mechanisms for safety.

A kitchen or bar stool placed in front of the island or countertop (I prefer those with a back for extra safety and support) enables mom or dad to prepare food there and have a place to rest should they need to sit down.

Cabinets

I don't understand why cabinets are hung so high. We get shorter as we age, making the shelves harder to reach. Odds are the cabinets in your parents' kitchen can't be lowered, but there are some modifications that can be done to make reaching them easier.

Let's start with the hardware. If projected hardware is preferred, consider using D-shaped handles. If flush hardware is desired, use large pulls with ample finger room. These are easier to grasp for those with decreased strength and mobility in their hands. If the hardware on the top cabinets is too high to reach, attach loops of rope or leather to the fixtures for mom or dad to grab on to and pull. Most housewares stores have lots of options for knobs and handles that can be easily switched in for the old hardware with nothing more than a screwdriver.

Cabinets can be retrofitted with pullout drawers. Some pull out and drop down to almost counter height. Lower cabinets can also be modified with pullout drawers so mom or dad doesn't have to bend down and reach in for what they need. There are so many options for organizing cabinets that I could not begin to list them here. One website I checked recently had over 1,300 items for sale under the heading "pantry and cabinet organizers." My favorites include accordion doors that pull out and hold tons of items, pullout spice and can racks, and shelving that positions pots and

pans on their sides to maximize space and ease of grasp. Lazy Susans can double the accessible storage space in corner cabinets.

The Kitchen Sink

The cabinet under the sink could be removed to allow mom or dad to be able to sit in front of the sink while they wash dishes or prepare food. Cover the pipes appropriately to avoid burning the legs (foam pipe insulation, available at hardware and home-improvement stores, works well for this). One of the best types of faucet has a single lever with a built-in anti-scald feature. These can easily be manipulated with one hand and provide a visual cue of the expected temperature of the water. A pullout spray faucet makes it easy to wash deep pots.

The Kitchen Table

Sitting down at the table—a seemingly simple task that was always taken for granted—is often problematic for many of my senior patients. At issue is pulling out the chair, maneuvering their body to get in position to sit, and then coordinating scooting the chair back under the table and actually sitting down.

Chairs that are on wheels can alleviate some of the maneuvering issues, but they need to be careful to guard against the chair slipping out from under them before they sit. The way to prevent this is to turn the chair so the back is against the table, sit down, and then turn to face the table while sitting on the chair. I also recommend this technique for sitting at a desk.

Furniture glides placed on the bottom of chair legs make sliding easier and also protect the floor. You can create homemade furniture glides by putting socks over each leg of the chair. If the chair is on carpet, plastic runners or mats most often used for offices can be placed under the chair to aid in movement.

Appliances

Appliances are the workhorses of the kitchen, and because they take up so much space and are such high-use items, they require special attention.

Refrigerator

The refrigerator requires the most frontal maneuvering to access. If possible, it should be located on a wall facing the most open and unobstructed area of the room. It is helpful to have counter space on each side of the refrigerator to place items. A side-by-side refrigerator-freezer is the easiest for everyone to access, including someone in a wheelchair. I recommend features such as ice and water dispensers on the outside of the door, long handles that allow for various gripping points, larger storage shelves on the doors, see-through bins, and slide-out shelves that make it easier to reach the food.

Stoves

An oven mounted 18 inches off the floor provides a convenient cooking height for someone who is sitting, while still being functional for a standing adult. Dials should be easy to read. As noted earlier, it's important to have a heat-resistant counter space next to the stove for safely transferring hot dishes out of the oven or off the cooktop.

Avoid the danger of reaching over hot burners by selecting cooktops with knobs that are in front or on one side of the stove rather than

along the back. If vision is a problem, consider outlining the knobs and marking the most-used settings with Hi-Mark pens. They create a raised, easy-to-see mark to delineate objects. They also work well on microwave dials.

If possible, consider installing a pot-filler faucet near the stove that folds out of the way when not in use. This reduces the need for transporting heavy pots of water from the sink to the cooktop and allows for easily adding in some water if it evaporates during cooking. To empty a heavy pot of water, slide it onto the counter and over to the sink. If you can't let the water cool, such as when making pasta, use tongs or a spaghetti scooper to lift the pasta out of the hot water and place in the colander. Another option is a rolling cart to transport it to the sink.

Toaster and Microwave Ovens

Many of my patients have given up using their ovens. Visual deficits make it difficult to accurately use the knobs, and weakness and joint abnormalities render it hard to lift pots safely out and up to the counter. Most dishes can easily be prepared in a microwave or even a toaster oven.

Toaster ovens take up little space and are relatively inexpensive. Besides toasting, they can be used for grilling, baking, and broiling. Why crank up the large oven when just preparing a meal for one or two? If mom and dad are still using their toaster oven from the sixties, replace it with one that has an automatic or timed shut off.

Microwaves are even more versatile, easy to manage, and also take up relatively little space. If possible, locate the microwave at counter height, and provide for adjacent heat-resistant counter space. Some of my patients have placed their microwave directly on the kitchen table so they can easily slide the cooked food right onto the table. To achieve the same effect, a rolling kitchen cart with a large-enough countertop to hold the microwave can be rolled over to the table when needed. The goal is to create a safe condition where it requires the least amount of steps to transport plates and bowls of food.

Dishwasher

The dishwasher should ideally be located on the side of the sink corresponding to the user's dominant hand. If your parents are a mixed lefty-righty marriage, maintain marital harmony by letting them figure out who's the main dishwasher loader. Ideally, install the dishwasher with the base 6 to 9 inches off the floor to reduce the need for bending. In older homes, however, this may not be possible due to an existing countertop.

Lighting and Power

Bright light is essential, especially in areas where food is prepared. Task lighting should be placed in appropriate areas such as over the sink, stove, and food preparation counters. LED lighting can be installed under high cabinets to increase the light on the workspaces.

Use a power strip on the counter to make it easier to plug in appliances if outlets are not within reach. If there is an island, consider having an outlet installed in it to plug in various appliances. Be careful to not overload any single outlet with plugs. Microwave ovens in particular should have their own outlet or they run the risk of tripping the circuit when used simultaneously with another appliance.

Declutter and Organize the Kitchen

With its cabinets full of cookware, drawers of utensils, and pantries stuffed with food, the kitchen is among the "busiest" rooms in the house. It also serves as the de facto "landing zone" for people when they enter the home, as evidenced by the piles of mail, sets of keys, eyeglasses, and other assorted items that tend to accumulate on every available surface. As such, it can often be the most daunting room to get a handle on.

Just like all the other rooms, the clutter in the kitchen can be tamed with a systematic, step-by-step approach. But before we begin . . .

A Word about Step Stools

You are probably thinking the word is "no" but actually it is "maybe." The first recommendation I made to Eunice about her kitchen was to put the cat food cans on a lower shelf of her cabinet, where she could easily reach them without climbing, along with other most-used items. But other things need to be tucked away on a higher shelf, like the special platter only used on Thanksgiving. Here is where a safe step stool may come in to play.

If you think mom and dad are "climbers" and nothing you say will change that, insist on a safe stool. This is better than having them climb on a chair or that old stool they saved with your name spelled out in block letters that you received as a baby gift. My requirements are a wide-based step with treads and a rubber bottom. Some have a safety bar handrail, like you may see in doctors' offices to help patients get up on the table. Also, one step is enough. Any more may cause issues with equilibrium. Avoid folding stools that have the potential to collapse.

Cabinet and Fridge Organization

Storage bins in the kitchen make it easier to put things away and eliminate clutter. To make items more reachable in closets and pantries, add a lazy Susan and sliding baskets or sliding shelves for things used most often. Place rarely used items in the deeper recesses of the cabinets.

When organizing items in the refrigerator, place things most often used in the front, on waist-level shelves, or in the doors. Some models come with convenient pullout shelving. Alternatively, various sized bins are available at home goods stores to help keep like items together and tighter on the shelf. The coldest part of the fridge is the bottom shelf in the back, so that is where to store raw meat that has been placed in a bin to catch any leakage. The middle shelf, which is generally at eye level, is the most accessible, so I recommend that location for the food that needs to be eaten soon, such as leftovers, plus things they use the most.

If mom or dad has arthritic joints or weakness in the hands and arms, they may have difficulty grasping and lifting large containers of juice or milk, yet they might insist on purchasing these quantities to take advantage of cost savings. To make it easier to pour the milk, buy small plastic containers with easy-access lids, and have someone transfer portions of the big container into the smaller ones to use throughout the week. The large containers can be placed way in the back where it is coldest to maintain their shelf life, and the small daily containers can be up front for easy access.

Food Preparation

I have become a fan of slow cookers (with auto shut off) for use by my senior patients. The ingredients can be thrown into the pot in the morning and taken out as dinner in the evening, with minimal monitoring, stirring, or maintenance.

Prepared foods and convenience items are helpful in decreasing repetitive movements that could lead to muscle strain in the arms and hands. Prewashed and shredded salad is a great example of this. Fresh vegetables are now being packaged in "stir-fry" packs, "roasting" packs, and "soup" packs, all precut and ready to go.

I have also found that a Keurig-type coffee maker is user-friendly for my patients. The water stays in the tank and needs only to be refilled a couple of times per week, and mom or dad merely has to place the coffee pod in the receptacle and press a button. I often suggest to the kids of my patients that this would make a great gift for the coffee- or tea-loving parent.

If mom or dad has any vision issues, suggest they use plastic, colored cutting boards for different foods to avoid cross-contamination. Use dark color boards for light foods and vice versa to create contrast.

An item called a rocker knife provides a sharp edge and cuts through thick vegetables or meat but does not require a lot of strength. If dad has arthritis or mom had a stroke, this knife is ideal because it can be used with one hand—it rocks over the food with a simple motion and does not require stabilizing the food with the other hand. Many other types of ergonomic kitchen tools are available with large, easy-grip handles. Oxo makes an amazing line of kitchen tools, from graters to salad spinners to utensils that can be found at places like Bed Bath & Beyond, Target, and Oxo.com.

Speaking of cutting with one hand, there are one-handed cutting boards that are designed with a couple of spikes coming up from the bottom to spear and thereby stabilize the food being cut. They also have a rim on the corners to stabilize the food for meal preparation. Picture placing a piece of bread in the corner of the board up against the rim and then spreading peanut butter on it with one hand.

Anything can easily be converted to "nonskid" by putting a rubber shelf liner under it. This helps keep bowls and appliances in place when working with them. Liners can be purchased at any home goods store in rolls that can be cut to any size.

Decluttering the Kitchen

As we did with the living areas in chapter 3, the first thing to do when planning on decluttering the kitchen is to throw out the obvious junk. This initial purge is a great way to get the motivation started and see fast results. A good place to start is the ever-present kitchen junk drawer. First get rid of the broken pencils, pens that have dried up, expired coupons, and various nails and screws that go to who knows what. Empty it totally, wash out the drawer, and put in a fresh liner. Many professional organizers say we should not have junk drawers, but I tend to differ. I love my junk drawer because it gives me a designated place to keep the little items that I need at any given time (e.g., pens that do write, paper clips, tape, twist ties, scissors, coupons that are not outdated). After you've tossed the bad junk, organize the remaining "good junk" by sorting related items into their own containers or draw dividers.

Next look at what is on the countertops and kitchen table with a fresh eye and evaluate which items really need to be sitting out there. Some appliances that are not often used, like a blender, might be better placed in a cabinet to free up precious counter space.

It is best when working on drawers and cabinets to tackle one at a time, but make the commitment to completely finish it. If mom or dad has a lot of items in the same category, you may want to help them decide which to keep. Confession time: I am attached to my huge set of pots and pans, even though I use the same soup pot, frying pan, and sauce pot over and over. So maybe you can let mom keep a couple more than you think necessary, but make it easy to reach the most-used cookware. After choosing the favorite pots and pans, check to be sure handles are fastened tightly and there are no cracks.

Same goes for kitchen tools, dish towels, and anything we tend to collect over the years. I discovered that I had six sets of measuring spoons, including a metal set, two plastic sets, and one that was heart shaped. Look at your accumulated items and categorize items into our five groups: keep, give away, sell or garage sale potential, charitable donations, and, of course, my favorite—the throw-away pile.

The pantry may be a project in itself depending on the size and the last time you tackled it. First, throw away all old or expired food. Most food items, even canned foods, have a "best used by date" imprinted on the label or can itself. Stocking up or buying in bulk may initially save money, but those savings will be lost if the food goes unused or has been around too long to still have the desired texture, flavor, and nutritional value. Determine what mom and dad use the most and put those items in the front of the pantry. An abundance of bins and shelf separators are available to increase storage space and make things in the pantry easier to spot and reach.

Hacks for Health and Home: The Kitchen

+ The kitchen sink is an option for those who have difficulty accessing the tub or shower and have become limited to sponge bathing. Place a tub chair in front of the sink to facilitate a nice sponge bath. Fill a spray bottle with warm water for a mini shower.

+ Bump dots provide a tactile clue for the visually impaired. They come in all shapes, sizes, and colors and stick on easily to almost anything, including the microwave, coffee maker, and other appliances. Research "bump dots" online for more information.

+ To transport items in the kitchen, my recommendation is for mom and dad to slide items along the counter rather than lifting and carrying them across the room. This is especially critical when dealing with heavy cookware or hot contents. Hopefully the counter is only a few steps from the table.

+ An old-fashioned, sturdy ironing board can be raised to the same height of the counter and used as a bridge between the counter and table.

+ After opening a jar of food, immediately mark the date on the label with a permanent marker before refrigerating it. This will save the angst of trying to determine how long it's been since it was opened and whether the contents are actually supposed to be green.

+ Clean the kitchen floor with a mop rather than on hands and knees. Push the mop forward and back rather than leaning too far forward, and clean small areas at a time. Don't fill the bucket too high—it will make it easier to dump and refill with clean water.

+ If they must scrub the floors by hand, have them kneel on a pad and not reach too far in any direction.

+ Use scissors to open packages rather than tearing with hands or teeth or attempting to cut open with a sharp knife.

+ Cut a small piece of rubber shelf liner and use it to open jars. Rubber gloves also work well.

+ Mount a fire extinguisher that is approved for grease fires in an easy-to-reach location. Review how to use it.

+ Place a pant hanger over a cabinet knob and use the hooks to hold a recipe.

- Out of counter space? Open a kitchen drawer and lay a cutting board over it.

- Use electric appliances to chop and blend rather than trying to do it by hand.

- Keep electric appliances safely away from the sink. Be sure power outlets near all water sources are GFCI (ground-fault circuit interrupter) outlets to prevent accidental electrocution.

- Remove cabinet doors if they impede access to contents. The downside of this hack is they have to keep it neat inside. Nobody wants to look at a messy jumble of cans, packages, and cartons every day!

- When preparing meals, double the recipe and freeze the extra portions for days when they don't feel like cooking. Label these freezer packets with their contents and date for no-guess reheating.

- Catch a break from washing and drying dishes by using disposable paper plates and plastic utensils.

- A wheeled cart in the kitchen is great for extra accessible storage and also helps with carrying food to the table and dishes back to the dishwasher or sink.

- A lazy Susan placed on the table lessens the need to reach for the salt, pepper, napkins, or, in my case, the reading glasses.

- A tool belt, garden tool belt, or apron with pockets is great to transport portable phones and other items around the kitchen, or anywhere else in the house for that matter.

- Jazz up your color scheme if vision is an issue or you just want to brighten things up. Yellow, oranges and reds are easiest to see. Use contrasting colors for dishes and tablecloths rather than, say, a white plate on a white cloth.

- For the person with cognitive impairment:

  - It may be necessary to remove the knobs from the oven to prevent them from using it and forgetting to turn it off. If necessary, shut off the stove completely at the main gas valve for a gas stove or at the circuit breaker for an electric one.

  - Consider placing knives and other sharp objects in a safe place out of sight.

  - Place a picture of what is in a cabinet on the outside so the person can easily find what they need without having to open several doors.

  - Use Post-it notes or a dry-erase board to write visual reminders of things mom or dad need to remember to do, such as "Turn off oven," "Take your pills," and "Close the refrigerator door."

CHAPTER 5

The Bedrooms

Anna said: My husband, Irving, carved the frame for our bed over sixty years ago. We slept in it together every night. He passed away last year and I miss him so much. I know my daughter is a bit worried because the bed is high, but I have never had a problem getting in or out of it. Well, once I did slip because I was reaching for the phone, but that is only because it was at the far corner of the night table. And the time I had a flare-up of my arthritis I had a little trouble getting my left leg up onto the bed. But otherwise I am absolutely fine.

Her daughter said: I want you to watch her get in and out of bed. It is very hard for her. She can barely get her legs up on the bed, and she actually fell out of bed reaching for the phone one night when I was calling to check on her. The bed is too high for the night table so she has a far reach to retrieve things. I have taken her to look at new beds, but she won't hear of it.

Lynda said: It is true that Anna had a hard time getting up onto her bed. The ornate wooden frame raised the mattress much higher than a regular bed, and she was fairly petite to begin with. I understood her attachment to the bed but explained that we needed to modify the situation or she was setting herself up for a fall. I had her daughter purchase from the local sporting goods store a step created especially for aerobics step exercises. It has sturdy rubber feet and a nonslip surface that is wide and easy to step up on. I taught Anna how to use the step to get onto the bed. I also recommended furniture risers for the night table so she could reach everything she needed throughout the night.

It's All About the Bed

It's called the bedroom because, well, it's dominated by the bed! So let's start there . . .

Position in the Room

When completing an assessment of my patients' ability to get in and out of bed, I take note of where the bed is located. Sometimes switching the side used for getting on and off the bed can shorten the distance to the hallway door or bathroom. That said, years of using a specific side of the bed can be a difficult habit to change.

Another navigational issue arises when the dresser is situated on the wall next to the bed. If mom uses a walker, try to create a pathway between the dresser and bed that is at least 36 inches wide to accommodate the walker. Expand that space to 5 feet if she needs to use a wheelchair. An alternative is for mom to "park" the walker near the foot of the bed and use the dresser to hold on to and guide herself to the head of the bed to sit down. If mom or dad doesn't use a device for walking, the dresser can still act as an aid to guide them as mentioned in chapter 3.

When your parents first set up their bedroom, chances are the bed was situated in the middle of the wall with the night tables equidistant from either side. The configuration that worked for a long time might not be optimal at this stage. One solution is to shift the bed a little bit one way or the other to make access easier for the parent in need. If there is only one person sleeping in the bed, you can create more accessibility by moving the bed farther over, possibly up against a wall, thereby creating a better pathway to access the bed from the desired side. Sometimes it merely takes a fresh eye to look at the placement of the bed and some simple tweaking to make a safer arrangement.

The Linens

Getting stuck in bed is a wintertime hazard—especially when pajamas stick to flannel sheets. Some linens are easier to move or slide on than others. So while flannel is warm, flannel pajamas on flannel sheets create friction that hinders mobility. Buy a nice cotton nightgown for mom and silk pajamas for dad, and the flannel sheets should be much easier to negotiate. Switching to cotton sheets will also ease mobility.

Another linen issue is the overflow of the bedspread or comforter gathering at the foot of the bed that could cause a tripping hazard. I always recommend to my patients that they do not let the bedspread drape across their walking path. Instead, fold extra bedding back toward the bed or tuck it, if possible, under the mattress.

Height of the Bed

Beds come in all types and sizes, just like the people who sleep in them. The height from the floor to the top of the mattress significantly impacts the ease with which one can get into the bed. The rule of thumb is the lower the height of the bed, the easier it is to get into. But here's the catch: the higher it is, the easier it is to get out of. Ideally, when your parent is sitting on the edge of the bed with knees bent at 90 degrees, their feet should rest flat on the floor. For the easiest transfers getting in and out of the bed, the height from the floor to the top of the mattress should be around 22 inches.

The bed frame, box spring, and mattress all impact the overall height of the bed. I have had patients finally treat themselves to a new mattress, only to be shocked that the "pillow top" has drastically changed the height of the bed and made it too high. On the other hand, well-worn beds are often too low. If it is too high they may have problems lifting their legs onto the bed, and if too low it may be too hard to push up to get off the bed.

So, Goldilocks, how do we make the height just right?

If a bed is too low, elevate it with risers that are available in most home goods stores and other retailers, including Target, Bed Bath & Beyond, and Staples. The risers are blocks that come in various shapes and sizes, are made of rubber or wood, and can increase the bed height from between 3½ to 7 inches. The risers should have a cavity in which the foot of the bed rests to ensure it doesn't slip off.

If the bed is too high, one option is to remove the rug rollers or wheels on the bed frame to effectively decrease the height by around 2 inches. Switching from a standard box spring to a shallow one could help compensate for a too-tall mattress. Other options would be to use a frame that eliminates the need for a box spring, or remove the bed frame and place the box spring and mattress directly on the floor. If the bed sits in a wooden frame and you know someone who's handy with tools, it may be possible to shave a couple inches off the bottom.

Getting On and Off the Bed

For a multitude of reasons, many falls occur when an elderly person stands up and starts to walk away from the bed.

One explanation is postural or orthostatic hypotension, medical names for low blood pressure caused by blood vessels that don't constrict when the body becomes upright.[1] This can result in dizziness or light-headedness. If mom or dad have fallen or struggle getting in or out of bed, I suggest an evaluation by their primary physician, who can assess for hypotension and make appropriate medical recommendations. The physician can also make a referral to an occupational and/or physical therapist, who can take a look and suggest a strengthening and mobility program, possibly coupled with recommendations for adaptive equipment and modifications in the bedroom.

I teach my patients to not plop down just anywhere on the bed. Instead, they should sit as close to the pillow as possible before lifting their legs onto the bed. This way, when they lie down and lift their legs, their head is near the pillow, their feet aren't hanging off the foot of the bed, and there's no need to hike themselves upward.

Transfer-handle bed rails are an effective modification to help the user move around in bed and to assist with sitting, standing, and balance before taking those first steps away from the bed. These devices are easily installed (my favorite three words: "no tools required"). Research "transfer-handle bed rails" for more information. Another device is a pivot bar, which is a tension-mount pole that fits between the floor and ceiling with a horizontal support to assist with standing and pivoting out of bed to a walker, wheelchair, or even a bedside commode. They are useful when the area next to the bed is narrow.

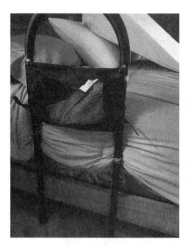

If mom is having difficulty climbing into bed because it is a bit too high, and if she has fairly good balance and mobility, the use of a step to lessen the gap between floor and bed can often do the trick, as it did for Anna. The key is to get the type of step that is used in step aerobic exercise. It must be wide, with a rubber nonslip bottom. They are often available with optional height levels. Another option is the Shure-Step stool (see the resources section for chapter 4).

If mom can sit on the bed but needs a bit of a boost to get her legs on, and if there is a bed frame, sometimes putting one foot on the frame and pushing off it may give her the lift she needs. This

works best with the wider wooden frames, but even the slight gap between the mattress and a metal frame creates a little space to put the heel of the foot on and get some leverage.

A leg lifter is a gadget that looks like a stiff dog leash with a loop at the end. Dad sits on the edge of the bed, shimmies his buttocks back as far as possible, catches his foot in the loop, and lifts his leg onto the bed.

Other Furniture and Bedroom Issues

The rest of the furniture in the bedroom should be arranged to allow for as many clear, straight, unobstructed pathways as possible. The most important path is from the bed to the bathroom. I will often come across a big, heavy dresser placed near the doorway (either leading to the hall or the bathroom) so that each time the patient wants to get through the door, she must walk around and "clear" the dresser. Slide it down the wall a few inches to eliminate these extra steps.

Check the drawers on the dresser to be sure they open easily. I have had patients fall backward struggling to open stuck drawers. A little WD-40 in the channels should do the trick.

The nightstand should be sturdy and of adequate size to hold important items that need to be easily accessible, such as a lamp, clock radio, phone, glasses, reading material, and flashlight.

Lighting

The best way to illuminate the bedroom during the day is by keeping curtains and shades open to let in natural light. Use the maximum wattage light bulb that is approved for their particular lamps. The bedside lamp should be easily accessible, and it should be easy to turn on and off. Install an illuminated rocker or touch light switch within easy reach from the bed. Rocker switches are easier to manipulate than standard switches and can be triggered with little manual dexterity using any part of their hand or even the elbow. A touch-sensitive or clapper-type lamp is a great modification for someone with diminished reach. A night-light should illuminate the path from the bed to the bathroom.

Flooring

I most often see carpet in the bedroom, which makes sense as this is the room where bare feet abound. I recommend a low pile. I am wary of shag carpets because they can snag walkers. If there are hardwood floors, any area rug in the room should be large and not move an inch when administering the Shrager twist test I described in chapter 3.

The Closet

A light switch right outside the closet that turns on an overhead light inside the closet will improve mom's ability to find what she is looking for, even if the closet is small. Closet rods hung at various heights make it easier to hang and retrieve long and short clothing. There are numerous do-it-yourself closet-organizing systems, or a professional closet-organizing company can analyze the needs of your parent and maximize space while ensuring ease of reach. Raised shoe racks can be purchased at any home goods store, and using them can relieve pressure on the back and knees by lessening the need to bend. A clear set of plastic drawers can be placed in the closet to organize belts, purses, scarves, and other accessories.

Getting Dressed

I discourage my patients from standing in the middle of the room to put on their clothes, but old habits are very hard to break. If the bed is an easy height to manage, that's the best place for mom and dad to put on their clothes. Dad can gather his clothing, lay it out on the bed, and then sit in a relaxed position to get dressed. When he stands to pull up his pants, in case he loses his balance, the worst-case scenario is that he falls back onto the bed. If the bed is too high, place a sturdy chair with arms against a wall in the bedroom to create another safe place to get dressed.

Declutter and Organize the Bedroom

Break down large tasks into smaller components that can be accomplished over time. Tackle the closet one day, change the linens on another, and save straightening drawers for a third day. Reorganize drawers when seasons change.

One of my favorite clothing tips is to get rid of any items of clothing that have not been worn in over a year. We often hope to shed a few pounds to be able to button those smaller-size pants once again, but it could be fun for them to treat themselves to something new when the waistline shrinks.

Donate clothes and other items to their favorite charity. They will feel better knowing others are benefiting from them, and they'll get a tax deduction to boot. If the clothing is especially vintage, consider donating it to theater groups. They're always looking for period clothing and accessories. You could also try to sell it at a consignment shop.

Hacks for Health and Home: The Bedroom

+ Be sure electrical and phone cords are running along the wall and not across any pathways.

+ If dad uses a urinal in the bedroom at night, place a plastic mat on the floor next to the bed. Be sure it is large enough and flat on the floor to not to create a slipping hazard.

+ Install a rail that your parents can hold on to that will lead them from the bed to the commode.

+ If the bedroom can't be safely accessed because it is upstairs, bring the bed down and set it up in the living or dining room. If their bed is too big, consider bringing down a smaller mattress— maybe from one of the other bedrooms.

+ The Mattress Genie is a really cool device that fits under the mattress and lifts it to various positions via remote control. It helps to prop up the person who has trouble breathing while lying flat or who may have back or hip issues.

+ Create positioning wedges out of foam to place under the neck, hips, or knees to reduce pressure and provide support as needed. You can find the foam at craft stores.

+ Group similarly colored clothing together (that is, blacks, blues, and navies), a tip that is good for everyone and great for people having trouble distinguishing colors.

+ Hang entire outfits on a single hanger (e.g., pants, blouse, and coordinating jacket).

+ Purchase drawer organizers to separate like items for easy retrieval.

+ If dad likes to empty his pockets onto the top of the dresser, a valet tray can hold all of his trinkets while decreasing the clutter there.

+ Over-the-bed tables are not just for hospital rooms. These provide a handy adjustable-height surface that can hold needed items next to the bed or in any room for that matter.

+ For the memory impaired, use automatic night-lights to illuminate the path from bed to bathroom.

CHAPTER 6

The Bathrooms

The son said (via text to my husband): Sorry to bother you on a Sunday, my friend, but I need some assistance. Actually I need help from Lynda. My dad was diagnosed this week with pancreatic cancer. We are waiting for the pathology results to see where we stand. My immediate concern is his safety. I stayed over at his house last night to assist him with going to the bathroom. My parents borrowed a toilet seat extension but it does not fit their toilet. And his walker is too wide to fit through the bathroom door. My mother is going to hurt her back hauling him on and off the toilet, and then we are all in trouble. They don't want anyone's help, but it's not a question of want, it's about safety. Please ask Lynda for her thoughts. The sooner she can get here the better. Thanks.

Larry said: I don't know why everyone is making such a big deal about this. I am fine. Okay, I'll admit to feeling a bit weak, but my son did not need to sleep over last night. My wife, Edna, can help me on and off the toilet.

Lynda said: The focus of my assessment was on the son's immediate concern about Larry safely using the bathroom without relying on Edna. Larry's walker was indeed too wide to go through the bathroom door, so I needed to create some adaptations to make the room safer. Following my recommendation, the son replaced the towel bar that was opposite the toilet with a combination grab bar/towel bar that would provide adequate support for Larry. I instructed Larry to park the walker at the door, walk through the threshold, and grab on to the new towel bar opposite the toilet. After assessing the toilet to determine whether the bowl was round or oblong, I ordered the correct type of raised seat, with handles on both sides. He could now walk in; grab the bar and turn; sit on the new, raised seat; and get up on his own. The son no longer needed to sleep over, Edna could get a full night's sleep, and Larry had his independence and dignity back.

Getting to the Bathroom

Sometimes just getting to the bathroom is a big hurdle, never mind using it. Most one-story homes will have at least one full bathroom containing a shower or tub. Two-story homes, especially those built more than a decade ago, generally have what is referred to as a "half bath" on the lower level that does not include a shower or tub. When I find one that does have a full bath on the first floor, I marvel at the forward thinking of the builder.

When a patient cannot make it upstairs to the tub or shower, whether that is the result of a long-standing or acute situation/diagnosis, I remind people to consider the kitchen sink for sponge baths and washing up. Often the downstairs bathroom is small, whereas the counter space in the kitchen is usually spacious enough to hold needed supplies and one can usually get close to the sink, even if in a wheelchair.

As far as toileting, if the actual toilet is difficult to access, the best alternative is to place a commode within a short distance of where the person spends most of their time. I often suggest placing the commode in the living room or den during the day if mobility or balance is impaired. This option is often met with resistance, at least at first. To afford privacy, I recommend the use of room divider screens, relatively inexpensive panels that can be purchased at Target, Walmart, and other large retailers. A small corner of the living room can become a bathroom in seconds.

A drop-arm commode, with arms that swing away, is a great piece of equipment to facilitate easier transfers to and from a bed, couch, or wheelchair. If situated in the bedroom, the commode can be placed right up against the bed. Even if the person can access the bathroom toilet, it saves multiple trips to the bathroom at night.

Doorways

With standard door widths between 28 and 32 inches, someone using a wheelchair or walker generally can gain easy access to the bathroom only if they are entering straight into the room. Larry's walker was extra wide to accommodate his size, and it simply was too big to fit through the doorway. To make matters worse, the actual bathroom was so small that even if he could have gotten the walker through the doorway, there was nowhere to put it. While a 36-inch-wide doorway would be ideal, such a renovation is impractical in most homes, this one included. However, some easy modifications might remedy the situation.

With most wheeled walkers, the two wheels protrude out from each side of the frame. If you remove the posts holding the wheels, switch them to the opposite legs, and reattach them, the wheels will then be on the inside of the frame. It should not hinder stability, and you will have gained 2 inches of room on each side of the walker. (Note: one exception would be that a larger person may not feel as secure with the narrower base of support.) For a tutorial on how to change the wheels in this manner, go to YouTube and search "How to Put Wheels on a Walker—Popular Home Medical Equipment."

To widen a door entrance without undertaking expensive renovations, one option is to try swing-away or swing-clear door hinges. These enlarge the doorway opening by 1½ to 1¾ inches, providing sufficient clearance for wheelchair entry. Another easy fix is to remove doorstops, those little "boingy" things behind some doors to keep the doorknob from hitting the wall. This will allow the door to open an additional three-quarters of an inch.

As a worst-case scenario, consider removing the entire door. This could add 2¼ to 2¾ inches of clearance. You can install a tension rod

between the doorjambs and hang a curtain that will just block the entrance, or install a curtain rod above the bathroom door that juts out a few inches either way and hang a decorative curtain that will cover the entire doorway and provide adequate privacy.

If remodeling, have the door open out rather than into the bathroom to provide more interior bathroom space. An outward-opening door is also a good safeguard because if a person falls in the bathroom in front of a door that opens in, it may be difficult to open the door to get to them. Pocket doors that slide into the wall and completely out of the way are a great option when remodeling or building a new home.

If the door cannot be widened in any way and dad must use a walker to get into the room, a technique called sidestepping works well. The person turns sideways at the doorway and, with the walker in front of them, takes one or two sidesteps and then moves the walker to catch up. They do this several times until they are through the doorway and can turn and face forward and continue walking.

Showers and Tubs

Okay, we're finally in the bathroom. The first thing I look at is the type of shower or tub. My worst nightmare is a claw-foot tub, which still exists in the old neighborhoods where many of my patients live. The best scenario is a walk-in, zero-threshold shower with the appropriate seating, easily reachable faucets, and grab bars around the entire perimeter, both vertical and horizontal. A girl can dream, can't she?

Size *does* matter, and the higher the tub walls the harder it is to get in and out. Some modifications can make it easier and safer to do so.

Grab Bars

My first inclination is to look for the best place to install a couple of grab bars. Grab bars come in all sizes, are available angled and straight, and are made of various metals and plastics. If using them inside the shower or tub, I highly recommend getting the textured ones that do not become slippery when wet. Generally speaking, a 24-inch vertical grab bar on either end to grab on to when entering the tub and a 36-inch horizontal grab bar across the back wall will suffice. It is amazing what a difference these grab bars will make. Mom and dad will feel so much more secure having something to hold on to while entering, exiting, and during the shower. Grab bars should be professionally installed into the studs in the wall.

For those who object to the often institutionalized look of basic grab bars, there are dozens of options on the market that are attractive, stylish, and very functional. A relatively new trend is a combination grab bar/soap holder, or grabs bars that double as towel bars. These products are made by such companies as Great Grabz, Invisia,

Grabcessories, and Moen and are available online and at home-improvement stores like Home Depot and Lowe's.

Grab bars that are bolted to the wall are the optimal choice, but bars that fasten to the wall with suction cups also have their place in the appropriate situations. For a suction grab bar to work properly, it needs to be applied to a smooth surface without any cracks or bumps, such as a fiberglass wall or on tile. If applying on tile, it cannot cover any grout lines, as this would break the seal and the suction cups will not adhere to the wall. They also work well on glass, smooth marble, and granite but never on a painted or textured surface where the grab bar will not stay attached and likely will pull the paint off the wall.

When using a suction grab bar, always remember it is there for balance but not for bearing weight. It must be taken down, cleaned, and checked for adherence on a regular basis. Suction grab bars are also ideal for figuring out the best placement for "real ones" that will eventually be installed. They can be moved around on the walls of the tub or shower and should adhere long enough to determine where to make a permanent, professional installation.

A bathtub safety handle can also be a helpful device for transfers into and out of the tub. This product consists of a vertical grab bar that rises from adjustable clamps that attach and lock to the wall of the tub. Because no tools are required (my favorite phrase!), installation is a snap. Some come in various heights to reduce the need for bending if mom or dad is tall. Note that some models are not recommended for fiberglass tubs.

I have had several patients who like to take a nice, long soak in the tub. Although that gives me a bit of angina, where there's a will there's a way. We need to think "outside the tub" and install grab bars low enough for them to reach when sitting on the bottom of the tub. The above-mentioned safety handle also works well here. Keep in mind that it is easier to get up from a surface when it is raised as much as possible. A simple fix is a bathtub pillow specifically made to sit in the tub to give you 3 or 4 inches of height above the tub floor. Waterproof seat cushions made for boats will also work well here.

Tub and Shower Renovations

Electronic bath lifts are easy to use and can make taking a "real bath" possible again. They are expensive, but to some they are well worth the investment. Check out the Bellavita Auto Bath Tub Chair Seat Lift by Drive Medical on YouTube to get an idea of how they work.

If mom and dad are dying to take a bath and you really want to go all out, you can get them a walk-in tub. The concept here is a high-walled bathtub with a door that opens and closes on the front wall of the tub. One enters the tub without having to step over the wall. Once inside and sitting on the seat, the door is locked and sealed and the water fills up, creating the experience of sitting in a bath. The good news is that it provides an option for those with mobility issues to continue to take a tub bath, with the luxury of bubble jets, handrails, and adjustable seating. The bad news is that they are expensive and must be professionally installed. And the patient must sit patiently in her birthday suit while the water fills up in the beginning and completely drains at the end. I'll let you ruminate on that one.

There is always the option of converting a walled tub into a shower, and numerous companies advertise the ability to complete this transformation in one to two days. Several of my patients have renovated their tub using this effective, albeit pricey, option. If mom and dad love the feeling of warm water pouring on them and can no longer get into the tub easily, this can be an effective modification to enable them to bathe safely. The renovation shown in the photo at the top of the next page took two days to complete and cost my patient $6,900.

Stall showers come in all sorts of styles and sizes. The best scenario is a walk-in shower with little to no threshold and grab bars installed at

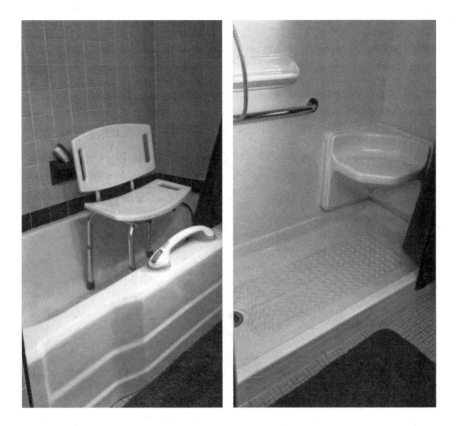

a height that works best for the patient. I like to see one hung vertically at the entrance and another horizontally across the back. I also recommend installing one outside the shower for support coming and going. (Not a bad idea for a tub, either.)

The biggest annoyance with zero-threshold showers is water slopping out onto the floor. Ideally, the floor is sloped back toward the drain so water won't spill out onto the bathroom floor, but that is not always totally effective. A long, weighted shower curtain will help to hold water in. There is also a product called a collapsible water barrier that can be placed along the edge of the shower to accomplish the same goal.

Remember simpler times when faucets simply turned water on, then off? Now there are many types from which to choose, some of which can be beneficial to those in need of some adaptation. The sprays can simulate a vigorous massage or the feeling of a tropical rainstorm.

Multifunction showerheads can provide an invigorating spray in the morning, a therapeutic spray after having worked all day, and a relaxing spray before bed.

My concern as a therapist is access to the faucet. Sliding-bar showerheads move up and down on a bar mounted on the wall and are beneficial because the height of the spray is easily adjustable. A handheld showerhead comes off the mounting and is most useful when washing hair or nooks and crannies, as I like to call the hard-to-reach parts. It is also a good choice when a caregiver will be helping with the shower.

Tub and Shower Surfaces

Flooring in the tub or shower is another area of potential concern, as it may be slippery. Many older tubs and showers were not produced with skidproof bottoms and become even more treacherous over time. Rubber suction mats can be purchased for the floor of the tub or shower, although many of my patients say they are tough to clean. One remedy is to clean the mat in your dishwasher. You would be amazed how practical that appliance is for cleaning so much more than just dishes.

There are also various roll-on coatings that can be applied to the bottom of a tub or shower. I like the peel-and-stick treads (fish-shaped are my personal faves), which are easy to apply and quite effective. Another easy product to install is the Gator Grip. It is a traction mat that is easily installed on the entire bottom of the tub. It does not have to be cleaned underneath because adhesive seals out mold and mildew. Check it out at noslipgatorgrip.com.

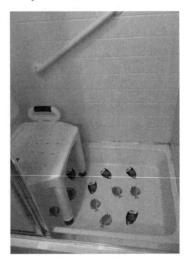

Seats for Showers and Tubs

Choosing the best of the many seat choices available will depend on mom and dad's physical needs combined with their type of shower or tub.

First, let me explain when to use a shower transfer bench versus a chair. A shower transfer bench is a long bench that is used to help transfer into the tub when the wall is high or when it is difficult for the user to raise her legs up over the wall. The outer two feet of the bench are placed outside of the tub and the inner two feet inside of the tub. The user backs up to the bench and sits down on the outer part, slides her torso along the seat and into the tub, and then lifts her legs over the wall. This alleviates the need to step over the tub wall, which is when many falls occur.

"But wait," you're thinking. "How does the water stay in during the shower if two legs are outside of the tub?" To keep water in the tub when using a transfer bench, use two shower curtains. Buy an inexpensive one to tuck inside the tub. Make a 24-inch slit up the middle where it meets the seat of the bench and then tuck it into the slots on the seat. This will keep the water in. A pretty, decorative shower curtain can adorn the outside of the tub. There is also a product called a BenchBuddy Hookless Shower Curtain that is made for this situation.

Unlike a shower transfer bench, a shower or tub chair is positioned with all four legs inside the tub. It does not help with the transfer in; rather, it is there to sit on if one does not have the endurance, strength, or balance to complete the shower standing up. I prefer chairs with backs for more support if there is room for them.

Many new senior housing projects feature magazine-worthy bathrooms with built-in fold-down seats in the shower/tub. Be wary of these, as my experience is that they never seem to be in the right place or at the right height.

Toilets

So much angst surrounds the use of this porcelain receptacle, and for good reason: when you gotta go, you gotta go! While traditional toilets measure less than 17 inches in height, most people have an easier time getting on and off toilets with a height between 17 and 19 inches. This is because as we age, our joints get creaky and our muscles get weaker and it is easier to get on and off a surface that is a bit higher. Newer construction almost always includes a "comfort height" toilet that is between 17 and 19 inches high, according to Americans with Disabilities Act (ADA) standards.[1] Rather than buy seat risers, many choose to replace their (often original) toilet with one that is a more comfortable height.

If the toilet is too low and you are not interested in totally replacing it, numerous products are available to help make it higher and safer. Raised toilet seats come with and without arms, and some have removable arms. The choice depends on both physical needs and allotted space surrounding the toilet. This would be a good time to consult with an occupational therapist to help you determine the best setup for your parents' needs.

Another issue to consider is the shape of the toilet bowl: round or oblong. Many seat-raising products are designed for one or the other. Most of the seats give a rise of 3½ to 4 inches. I would not recommend anything higher, as it might be a hindrance for shorter people. (It's not fun to have a stomachache or try to enjoy the Sunday *Times* on the throne with your feet dangling in the breeze.)

Although raised toilet seats can be very helpful, some of my patients complain that the opening is too small, which may lead to difficulties completing personal hygiene after a bowel movement, and often there is no lid because the actual lid of the toilet stays up to accommodate the riser. An alternative to adding a riser is a product called the Toilevator, which raises the entire toilet on a plastic base installed into the floor. It was researched and developed at the Centre for Studies in Aging, which is a division of Sunnybrook Health Sciences Centre in Canada. It adds 3½ inches of height to either a round or oblong toilet, and the biggest perk is mom continues to be able to sit on the actual seat of the toilet.

If you do not need added height, you can just add handles on either side of the toilet. An example of this setup is a product called a Versa frame. This is an armrest that surrounds the toilet to provide a gripping surface to help push up off of and lower down onto the toilet without adding height to the seat. Pull-down bars, also called flip-up bars, attach to the wall with tension adjustments so they can be set to various heights depending on the needs of the user. They need strong support in the wall in order to remain sturdy, so have them installed by someone familiar with this type of work. When not in use, they fold up against the wall and out of the way. They're like the Murphy bed of grab bars!

Larry, my patient from the beginning of the chapter, elected to use a raised toilet seat with arms to help him in the bathroom. He could walk into the bathroom as discussed earlier, grab on to the grab bar on the wall, turn and grab the arms of the newly installed raised toilet seat, and safely sit down. When finished he was able to easily use his arms to push up from the toilet without any help. His son did not have to sleep over to help his dad use the toilet, and his wife did not have to get up.

If there is not enough space on either side of the toilet for a seat with attached bars or a Versa frame, a grab bar on the wall next to the toilet may be an option. My patients often ask me how to position it—horizontally, vertically, or at a slant. At issue here are the person's needs and limitations. The goal is to achieve the proper leverage. This is where an OT can be very helpful by assessing the patient's range of motion and strength in order to recommend the best placement of the bar(s). Another option to facilitate rising from the toilet is to place a grab bar on the wall opposite the toilet to provide leverage for pulling straight up.

One of my favorite new products is a combination grab bar/toilet paper holder. It is attractive, does not look like a grab bar, and has a weight capacity of 250 pounds.

Sinks

The ideal sink height is one where the basin and fixtures can be comfortably reached whether standing or seated in a wheelchair. Generally, a 30-inch-high vanity top provides good access if seated. A height of 30 to 34 inches is an ideal standing level for people of varying heights.

Someone in a wheelchair needs approximately 27 to 30 inches of room under the front of the sink to pull up close enough to reach the basin. Many older homes have cabinets under the sink that may make access difficult. Possible remedies include removing the doors of the cabinet to allow room for one's legs to get under, or removing the whole cabinet and replacing it with a decorative curtain. Keep in mind that you need to protect the legs from any sharp edges or hot water pipes that were previously shielded by the cabinet.

Many of my patients tend to lean heavily on their sinks when completing their grooming and hygiene activities. It is important to ensure that this common practice does not result in damage to the sink or

injury to the patient. It might be helpful to install a grab bar under the front edge of the sink for safety and an extra support brace from the sink to the wall to ensure it doesn't pull out.

Single-lever faucets are best because they provide a visual indication of water temperature from a single tap and don't require fine hand dexterity to operate.

Flooring

If your parents are completing a bathroom renovation or buying a new home, install nonskid or slip-resistant flooring in the bathroom. Most of the time we have to work with the existing flooring. People are often reluctant to use bath mats because they "heard" you should remove all throw rugs to prevent falls, but in this case I advise otherwise. In the bathroom, I recommend a good-sized rubber-backed rug in front of the tub or shower to step onto after bathing. This helps to dry the feet, and any water dripping off you is absorbed rather than making the floor slippery.

One frequent problem I observe is that patients have the same bath mat they purchased when they first moved in twenty years ago. I promise you that the rubber on the bottom has deteriorated over time. If you don't believe me, go into mom's bathroom and try the Shrager twist test. Stand with both feet planted firmly on the rug and try to do the twist. If the rug moves, throw it out and treat them to a new one.

Declutter and Organize the Bathroom

Take a fresh look at the bathroom and see if any decluttering and orga- nizing can give mom and dad more room to navigate while still enabling them to easily reach the most often used items. This begins, as it does with all rooms in the house, with throwing away any nones- sential items. Look through the drawers and medicine cabinet and get rid of expired drugs, seldom or never-used items, and almost-empty bottles of shampoo, cream rinse, and moisturizers.

Most of the older homes that my patients live in seem to have small bathrooms. Storage bins and baskets can help immensely to contain items like toiletries and medicines while providing easier access. They can be placed in cabinets, situated neatly on a countertop, or even tucked away on the shelves of the linen closet. Note how this person labeled the various receptacles in the photo below so her husband could easily find needed supplies. My favorite is the bearded man that offers the visual prompt for his shaving supplies. Consider using any available vertical space to hang shelves, such as above the toilet, for increased reachable storage.

Organizing the linen closet is gratifying but challenging, because there is so much folding involved. Folding, however, is a great exercise for my patients, as it requires them to move all the joints of their arms but with little resistance. Put mom in front of the table with a pile of towels and sheets and let her go to work. Separators that adhere to the shelf are wonderful to keep the piles of folded towels and linens from falling over. This is also a good time to dispose of sheets and towels that have seen better days. Suggest mom and dad treat themselves to some new linens with high thread count and soft, absorbent cotton towels.

Organize medicines by gathering all the expired ones and throwing away any that are past their prime. Prescription medicines have expiration dates on the labels; dates for over-the-counter meds are stamped on the bottles and boxes. Be sure to follow the specific disposal guidelines on the bottle or patient information sheet. Don't flush prescription drugs down the toilet unless directed to do so. Check for hazardous waste collection sites and "take back" programs that allow you to bring in unused drugs for proper disposal. If in doubt about what to crush, flush, or throw away, you can always ask the pharmacist for advice. Remove identifying information from the prescription label before disposing to help maintain your parents' privacy and protect personal health information. You don't need the world to know they have acid reflux, are diabetic, or need a little something to take the edge off of that depression.

Items that may need to be moved out of the way include the bathroom scale—there's no rule that it must be in the bathroom—and the wastebasket and clothes hamper. Keep a set of cleaning supplies as well as a toilet bowl brush and plunger in all bathrooms to eliminate the need to transport them from room to room. Use long handles for mops, brooms, and dustpans to avoid bending. For bathtub cleaning, mom or dad should stand outside the tub with a long mop rather than sitting and leaning over the side while scrubbing with a sponge.

Regarding access and safety, grab bars are not just for tubs and showers. I have recommended that patients place suction grab bars on the countertop next to the sink so they can hold on to something while brushing their teeth, shaving, or washing up. Remember not to adhere them to a surface that is bumpy or has breaks or grout lines, as they simply will not attach. Regular grab bars can also be installed on the wall just inside the doorway, as shown in this photo, which is especially handy when a walker must be parked outside the room.

Hacks for Health and Home—The Bathroom

+ Sliding glass doors on a tub preclude the use of a transfer bench and often make it difficult for a caregiver to reach in to help their loved one. Consider removing the doors and putting up a tension rod with a shower curtain. If the need for easy access into the tub is not chronic, or if you ever need to sell the home, the doors can be easily put back in place if you don't remove the tracks. This also works well for a shower with a glass door.

+ Be very careful when using powder. It turns the bathroom floor into an ice-skating rink. Only apply when standing on your amazing new rubber-backed bath rug, or save it for when you go into your carpeted bedroom.

+ Great present idea: a thick, thirsty terry cloth robe to put on after bathing. It will absorb most of the moisture, making drying off easier.

+ We all know that the job is not over until the paperwork is done. I can't begin to tell you how many of my patients have trouble reaching behind to wipe themselves. If that describes your parents, know that they are not alone. Consider a portable bidet attachment for the toilet that can help clean hard-to-reach spots. Also, there are extended-reach handles for toilet paper. Research "extended reach toilet paper aid."

- While we're on the subject of wiping, thick, disposal baby wipes are easier to handle and do a better job than regular toilet paper.

- If your parents have a tub seat, think outside the box (or tub in this case) and place it in front of the sink to complete their morning and evening wash up routines. The seat gives them a firm, safe, waterproof surface to sit on if they feel tired or weak. Purchase an inexpensive tilting makeup mirror and place it in the space between the faucet and the wall so they can see their face and upper body while sitting.

- Always have a night-light on in the bathroom to safely illuminate the way for those nighttime visits.

- Use a shower caddy to hold all needed items in one reachable place. You can hang it off the shower chair or bench or suction it to the wall.

- Body washes that come in pump bottles are easier to handle than a bar of soap. Use a loofah-type sponge that comes with a strap that goes around the wrist to ensure an easy grip. Squeeze on a few drops of body wash to create a nice lather.

- Put a rubber band around the slippery shampoo bottle to improve grip. You can also put multiple rubber bands on the cream rinse to help tell it apart from the shampoo. Better yet, transfer these products to pump bottles so they can be operated with only one hand.

- If they have trouble reaching all parts of their body, purchase long-handled brushes for washing legs, back, and feet.

- Foot scrubbers are great gadgets that adhere to the floor of the tub with suction cups. They have upward-facing bristles that remove rough and dry skin like a loofah and clean the feet just with a wiggle of the toes. All mom has to do is rub her feet along the brush's surface.

- Neither the top of the shower door nor the towel racks are grab bars and may not hold you if you begin to fall. Do your parents a favor and install the real thing.

- If a tub chair is not available, an all-plastic chair that people often use to sit on outside can work in the tub.

- If there is room for it, place a regular chair in the bathroom for dad to rest on and dry himself when he steps out of the tub. If there is no room for this, sitting on the toilet to rest and dry oneself also works.

- For the person with memory impairment:

  - Remove locks from bathroom doors so they can't lock themselves in.

  - Wastebaskets may need to be moved out of sight, as they can be mistaken for a toilet.

  - Electric razors are the safest to use.

- Here is my favorite bathroom tip that my patients who favor bar soap love the most. Take a lady's stocking or pantyhose and cut a leg off. Place a bar of soap in the foot and tie the "soap on a rope" to the towel bar or grab bar in the tub or shower. They can wash themselves right though the stocking and never drop the soap again!

CHAPTER 7

The Stairs, Hallways, Basement, and Laundry

Kate said: So, Lynda, here you are again. About a week after you discharged me from home care, I was in the kitchen and tried to walk across the room without my walker. I know you said I needed the walker, but I wanted to see how I would do. Well, I let go of the walker, turned toward the refrigerator, and boom, I was on the floor. I went through surgery for a broken hip and three weeks of in-patient rehab. I so badly want to get up the stairs to take a shower.

The grandson said: We moved the bed downstairs into the dining room. Once or twice a week we come over, she tells us what clothes she needs, and we go up and get some outfits for her. She is doing the best she can with sponge baths in the tiny downstairs bathroom, but she is really dying to get upstairs. We hope you can help her.

Lynda said: Kate is one of my repeat patients who I fondly refer to as a frequent flyer. She has had several falls and has now had both hips replaced. The scene at her house is typical for a patient after a fall or a fracture, surgery, or worsening of a disease causing weakness and difficulty walking. Her grandsons moved her bed downstairs to the dining room and set up grandma as best as possible until she can again negotiate the stairs.

Kate's home therapy program consisted of occupational and physical therapy. As the occupational therapist, I facilitated the installment of an additional banister going up the other side of the stairs, as Kate needed to use the strength of both arms for support, balance, and to pull herself up. We also extended the banister along the wall at the top

landing so that Kate had something stable to hold on to as she reached for her walker to turn toward the bathroom.

Stairs

Stairs are often the biggest hurdle to aging in place. They are the bane of existence for the therapist, the caregiver, and mostly the seniors.

Treads and Risers

Here is a quick review of the makeup of a step, which I covered in chapter 2 when discussing exterior stairs. The tread is the horizontal part that your foot steps on. The riser is the vertical height of each step. Closed risers are those with a vertical surface between the steps that your toe touches, as opposed to open risers, which are more common with outdoor decks and winding staircases. The height of risers and treads should be standardized according to local municipal building codes.

To assess the safety of your parents' staircase, check that risers are a maximum of 7 inches from one step to the next. Lower risers are even better. The tread should ideally be 11 inches deep so that the entire foot can fit on it straight-on. Open risers create a tripping hazard that can be eliminated by installing a piece of wood in the space.

The construction of older homes is "grandfathered in" and is not required to meet the latest building codes. Without a complete renovation, changing the shape of the staircase is generally not an option. However, if you or your parents are considering a renovation, or if you are looking to build a new house or purchase an existing one, keep in mind the type of stairs that can help with aging in place. For example, straight staircases at least 36 inches wide are best for adding a banister or installing a stairlift.

Railings

To increase staircase safety, install railings on both sides and extend them past both the top and bottom steps. The transition from the last step onto the landing can be difficult, and the extended railings offer extra support in both directions.

The railings should be installed 1½ inches away from the wall so mom's knuckles aren't scraping against the wall. A rounded railing between 1¼ and 1½ inches in diameter is the optimal shape and size for grasping. Some of the flat, ornate iron rails or those made of antique mahogany are beautiful, but they are wide and thick and often are hard to effectively hold on to.

Flooring

One type of floor is as safe as another, as long as the flooring is in good repair and not slippery. Shoes or slippers with rubber bottoms, socks with rubber skids on the bottom, or even bare feet are generally safer than wearing regular socks on wooden staircases. Many people feel safer having a carpeted staircase, but look for holes or portions that have frayed from years of wear and tear. Some of my patients who don't have wall-to-wall carpeting have opted for a carpeted runner. The lower the pile, the easier it is to navigate. Another option is to install tread tape that comes with a peel-off backing and can be placed on each step to provide traction.

Visibility on Staircases

Good lighting is essential on staircases. As we age, our vision gets worse and it becomes more difficult to discern where one step ends and the next begins. Light switches should be installed at both the top and bottom of the stairs. Steps are easier to see with a contrasting color along the edge of each tread. This can be accomplished by painting the edges of the steps or applying traction or duct tape along the edges.

I recently conducted a residential assessment for a new client who was determined to age in place in his 102-year-old home. The carpet on the stairs was close in color to that of the floor, making it harder to safely see where one surface ended and the other began. He is legally blind and had placed duct tape along the edge of the tread of the bottom step so he "could find the stairs." I pointed out that this could potentially be a slippery hazard, and he noted that he understood that and was very careful. Thus far his modification has been working out just fine. Often my patients create the best and most inexpensive "hacks."

Sunken Rooms

Sunken rooms come in and out of architectural fashion. Both my in-laws' past home and my own current home coincidently sport a room that requires navigating a couple of steps to get in and out. Where my patients are concerned, sunken rooms are a fall waiting to happen. Modifications are essential.

In my own home, the two wooden steps leading down to the sunken living room have no contrast on the edges of the tread and therefore are easy to miss. After a couple of guests stumbled, my short-term fix was to place colored painter's tape along the edges to help guests detect where the stairs begin.

My mother-in-law had developed severe arthritis over the years, to the point where she could not safely negotiate the two steps leading from her kitchen down to her den without fear of falling. Thankfully my handy brother-in-law built a beautiful banister, which made all the difference. She felt safer and more confident going in and out of the den, and the modification fit in with the room.

When the steps leading to a sunken room are very wide, consider installing one banister down the side and another closer to the middle (as seen in the above photo) so mom can grab them with both hands simultaneously. If a banister is not a realistic option, consider installing a grab handle on the walls on either side of the steps for mom to grab on to on her way up and down.

Stairlifts

Stairlifts can be a game changer, as they can often make the difference between being able to stay safely at home and needing to consider other housing alternatives. It's easiest and least expensive to install them on straight staircases, but they can be customized to accommodate most designs, including winding staircases and those with landings. When the seat is in the final position at the bottom or top of the stairs, it can be hazardous getting around it. Note how the stairlift in the photo not only accommodates a winding staircase, it also circles around and back behind the staircase rather than "landing" at the bottom of the stairs.

One of my most interesting patients was an 87-year-old man who was determined to stay in his four-story brownstone, which was built in 1890. This was the quintessential depiction of aging in place. When he purchased the home in the 1980s, there was a stairlift already installed that, according to its owner, may be the oldest working stairlift in existence. The seat on this stairlift is a rich leather nailhead, and the track winds three times up the mahogany staircase.

For someone who cannot transfer into a regular chairlift, an inclined platform lift is an option. It is designed to carry wheelchair users up a flight of stairs.

Other Options for Getting from One Level to Another

If the house has two closets that are stacked on top of each other, it may be possible, albeit costly, to install an elevator shaft in the combined open space. A new type of elevator uses a pneumatic lift through a hole in the ceiling to accomplish the ride from one floor to the next. These are great, as they don't require the stacked closets. Some look like futuristic glass tubes—think, "Beam me up, Scotty."

Elevators can also be installed on the exterior of the house. This would require construction of a door leading inside. Research "residential elevators" for more information, or go to YouTube for a video presentation.

Hallways

Hallways should be at least 36 inches wide. Those that are 42 to 48 inches wide are much easier for someone in a wheelchair, as it allows them to turn and more easily maneuver through a bedroom or bathroom doorway. Install a light at either end of the hall for maximum safety. Many of my patients, especially those with longer hallways, try to protect the flooring by covering it with throw rugs and runners. I always encourage them to look at the condition of those coverings to make sure they are not frayed and that the backing will safely stay in place and not create a new hazard.

An easy modification in a wide hallway is to add a railing along one of the walls. We tend to think they only belong on staircases, but in fact a railing placed in a long, poorly lit hallway can provide support and security, especially for those late-night "runs" from the bedroom to the bathroom.

Thresholds

The transition between two rooms in a home can be a trouble spot for mom and dad. Watch as they walk from room to room and note how they do when traversing the thresholds. A change from carpet to wood or other type of flooring can be visually confusing, even if the threshold is low. While a flush interior threshold is preferable, it should not exceed 1/4 inch of height. Anything higher can cause a tripping hazard for someone with weakness in the legs or poor balance. Modifying the thresholds in a home is usually an easy project and can be accomplished using various types of materials, including wood, tile, marble, and aluminum. The lower and smoother the threshold, the better.

Basements

Speaking about the bane of everyone's existence, let's add basements to the list. I am discussing it here because most often the hazard is the stairs and not the basement itself, which one of my physical therapist colleagues affectionately refers to as the dark hole of death. These staircases are often not finished and have open treads. If there is a banister, it often does not safely cover the entire length. Yet mom insists on going up and down the stairs to store or retrieve items from the basement or, even worse, to do the laundry, lugging a laundry basket to boot.

Although you might not be able to discourage those trips down to the basement, at least consider installing carpet on the steps, banisters on both sides, and light switches at the top and bottom. If it is not a finished basement, the stairs are most likely made of stone or wood. By making the recommended modifications (carpet or a runner, banisters, and lights), you will at least have created a safer situation. If you're desperate, go the guilt route by telling her you can't sleep at night because you keep picturing her in a heap at the bottom of the stairs.

The above-mentioned physical therapist was completing an assessment when she came upon a door. "The basement, I assume?" she asked.

"Oh, yes, but we never go down there," her patient assured her.

"May I open it to see what you've got there?" She opened the door to reveal an old stone staircase with a huge pile of empty plastic water bottles at the bottom. The patient explained that she and her husband drink several bottles of water every day and toss the empties down the stairs, creating a cushion that, if need be, would break their fall. They had gotten the idea from seeing children jumping into ball pits at McDonald's. You can't make this stuff up.

Laundry

If the washer and dryer are set up in the basement, suggest moving them somewhere upstairs to make it easier to continue to do their laundry while also eliminating the hazard of transporting the clothes between floors. I have had my patients relocate them to a main floor bathroom, into a corner of the kitchen, out to a heated garage, or even up to the second floor. If they can move the washer and dryer to the second floor, it would eliminate negotiating any stairs in the pursuit of clean clothes. I recommended that one of my patients install them in a closet in the guest room that backed up to the bathroom and was accessible to necessary plumbing. If space is an issue, regardless of where the laundry is relocated to, mom may have to transition to a stackable washer/dryer combination. Any of the remedies are preferable to taking a fall on the basement steps.

If they are able to remodel the laundry room, create adequate space surrounding the appliances to enable easy access for a walker or wheelchair if needed. Front-loading washers and dryers are also the easiest to use for loading and unloading clothes. When placing full-sized appliances side by side, make sure the one on the left opens to the left and the one on the right opens to the right, making it easier to switch the clothes from the washer to the dryer.

Perhaps as a gift, you could get your parents a gift certificate to a dry cleaner or laundromat that picks up and delivers regular laundry.

Hacks for Health and Home: Stairs, Halls, and Laundry

+ Place a colored strip of tape or paint the edges of steps to more easily see where each step begins and ends.

+ Keep a consistent light level in bedrooms and hallways, and use night-lights to guide mom from the bedroom to the bathroom.

+ For patients who need a walker, get one for each level to avoid the dangerous task of transporting them up or down the stairs.

+ Remember Antonio from chapter 1 who insisted on doing laundry in the basement? I taught him to swap the laundry basket for a drawstring laundry bag like the kind kids take to college (a pillowcase or plastic garbage bag will work, too) and use the following techniques:

- Tighten the drawstring or tie the top of the pillowcase and toss the laundry down the stairs. Slowly and carefully walk down, holding on with both hands, then grab the bag at the bottom and do the laundry.

- When the clothes are dry, place them back into the bag and drag the bag up with one hand while holding on to the banister. The clothes will not wrinkle during the two-minute journey up the steps. Back on the main floor—or better yet, in the bedroom, where most of the clothes belong—is the place to fold the clothes and put them away.

- Another option for transporting laundry is to use a large plastic bag like the recyclable shopping bags with long handles that can be placed over one shoulder, keeping both hands free for holding on to the railing.

CHAPTER 8

General Tips

The preceding chapters analyzed the most common residential challenges facing aging seniors who want to remain in their own homes, along with suggestions for solving them. In this chapter we look at several general issues applicable to various locations throughout the house and also some everyday tasks that frequently put seniors at risk.

Monitoring from Afar

If they are agreeable to it, obtain a personal emergency response system (PERS) for your parents to wear so that with the push of a button, an alert can be issued to a twenty-four-hour call center if they are in need of help. These devices can provide a variety of services, are sold or leased by numerous companies, and can be worn either on the wrist or hanging around the neck. Some versions are programmed to sense a sudden change in position and will signal an alert if the senior should fall, even if the button is not pushed. Many patients initially believe they do not need this sort of device, but they tend to change their minds after one fall. Tell mom to think of it as an important piece of jewelry that's as much for your peace of mind as hers.

Today's new smart technology provides a range of options for keeping an eye on mom and dad. I highly recommend having the "Big Brother" discussion with them before implementing any of these strategies to respect and maintain a balance between your need to know how they are doing and their right to privacy. Finding common ground on this issue can provide peace of mind for both you and them.

One simple way to visually communicate from a distance is by using Skype. It is a free software application that enables you to use the internet to make voice calls and/or see each other via a live video. It will work on your smartphones, tablets, and computers, and the download and set up is relatively easy. It is also a fun way for mom and dad to see various family members or old friends who don't live near them. From a caregiving perspective, it is a great way to communicate with your parents and allow you to look directly at them no matter where they or you are in the world.

Sensor monitoring systems consist of small wireless monitors that are strategically placed around the house to detect change in activity patterns. For example, if mom regularly gets up at 8:00 a.m., makes a pot of coffee, opens the refrigerator to get some cream, and turns on the TV to watch the news, you would be able to detect if all of this happens via the sensors. If she walks into the bathroom but does not come out, that would be indicated. The system sends the caregiver a message via phone, text, or email alerting them that something is unusual. See the resources section for this chapter in part 3 for information on some of the more popular systems.

Camera monitoring systems (now we're really talking "Big Brother") will allow you to have a visual connection with mom and dad. Cameras are placed in various key locations in the home, and a live real-time video can be seen from afar via a mobile device or computer.

Safety

Remind your parents not to carry too many items when entering, exiting, or moving around the house. Better to take more trips. Carrying too many objects in their arms will obstruct their vision, and trying to retrieve fallen objects creates the risk of a fall. One remedy for the latter issue is to purchase a reacher/grabber to assist in picking up fallen objects. Long barbecue tongs can also accomplish the task without bending down. See the list of hacks below for more ideas.

Set the hot water heater to 120°F to avoid unintended scalding. Unplug small appliances such as toasters, toaster ovens, and coffee makers when going away. Regularly clean the lint trap on the clothes dryer, as accumulated lint is highly flammable and decreases the effectiveness of the appliance.

Install fresh batteries in smoke and carbon monoxide detectors. One way to remind mom and dad to do so is to purchase a large calendar, hang it in a prominent location, and make a notation on their birthdays to switch out the batteries. As hearing or vision declines, you can install audible and visual strobe light indicators to warn them when a smoke or CO_2 detector is activated, or to let them know when the phone or doorbell is ringing. Discuss a house escape route for mom and dad with a few possible options. Be sure they actually practice it.

Make a video of the contents of their house in case of fire or robbery. Simply move from room to room with a smartphone or video camera to make a record of important possessions. Then download the video, save it to an inexpensive portable thumb drive, and store that drive in a safe place outside of the house.

Clothing

Believe it or not, the clothing mom or dad wears can impede their ability to move around safely.

Start by ensuring their footwear is compatible with their activity. So many of my patients walk around with tattered old slippers with no treads. Some have difficulty putting on shoes because of swollen feet. Socks with treads are a good option here. A brand called Dr. Comfort has a large variety of stylish shoes geared toward those with medical conditions, including diabetes and edema. Many come with Velcro straps to eliminate the need to tie laces with aged, less-nimble fingers.

Remind them to be wary of the length of their clothing. Pajama pants, bathrobes, and nightgowns in particular can be tripped on if they are too long. The same goes for long sleeves—they can be a hazard if too long, especially while cooking over a hot stove.

Fabric matters, too. Flannel pajamas on flannel sheets create resistance and preclude easy mobility in bed. Some of my patients spent sleepless, uncomfortable nights caught up in their sheets before learning to avoid flannel-on-flannel. (See chapter 5 for details on what to wear to bed.)

Pets

Most experts agree that the benefits of owning a cat or dog far outweigh the risks. Walking a dog provides cardiovascular exercise, and studies have shown that pet ownership can lower blood pressure and stress levels. Having a pet in the home has been shown to alleviate depression and loneliness for some seniors.[1] My personal experience definitely backs that up.

That said, the Centers for Disease Control and Prevention (CDC) publicized the results of a first-of-its-kind study looking at the incidences of pet-related injuries. The report found an estimated 86,629 fall injuries related to pets, and people 75 years or older experienced the highest rate of injuries.[2] Most of the injuries occurred in or around the home as a result of tripping over the pet or its paraphernalia. A smaller percent occurred when the person was walking their dog. Most cat incidences involved tripping over the cat or while chasing after it. And remember Eunice in chapter 4, who fell climbing for a can of cat food that was out of reach? Puppies can be a risk because they tend to fall asleep quickly wherever they are, while old dogs may fall asleep in precarious locations such as at the top or bottom of a flight of stairs, in dark hallways, next to the bed, or at their owner's feet. Most falls associated with pets are preventable once we are aware of the potential hazard.

Share the following tips with mom and dad so they can have safe fun with Fido and Felix:

+ Place food and water bowls out of the way of traffic. If they have a dog that slobbers when she drinks, place bowls on large, absorbent mats, and try to wipe up water on the floor as soon as it appears.

+ Use a long-handled pooper-scooper to clean the cat's litter box to avoid bending over. Scoop the poop into a large, lined wastebasket while standing upright.

+ Do like I do and keep dog toys in big wicker baskets both upstairs and down. (She refuses to pick up after herself!)

+ Be aware of your pet's location, especially when walking in dark hallways and at night. Place a bell on their collar so you can hear where they are, or use a glow-in-the-dark collar that recharges in daylight. Many pet stores sell an inexpensive combination bell/glow-in-the-dark collar.

+ Train your pet to tolerate being placed in a crate for those times when they may be underfoot or excitable, such as when company comes.

+ My dog rushes downstairs with me when the doorbell rings. Stop and let them go first.

+ All dogs should know the commands "sit" and "stay" and should be taught not to jump on mom or dad.

+ They should also be taught good leash manners, including not pulling, lunging after other dogs or people, or cutting in front of the person walking them. There are different types of collars or soft leash–type restraints to help keep your dog safely by your side.

Hacks for Health and Home: General Tips

Here are a few general tips that mom and dad can use to help adapt their surroundings as their physical abilities decline.

+ Shoe holders that fit over a door are not just for shoes. Here are some other ideas for them:

  ▸ In the bathroom the pockets can hold the hair dryer, hair clips, extra toilet paper, and first aid and medical supplies.

  ▸ In the bedroom, they become convenient holders for underwear, socks, and belts.

  ▸ In the laundry area, they store detergent, cleaning supplies, hangers, and extra chargers and cables.

+ Rubber shelf liners have many uses beyond their stated purpose. For instance:

  ▸ Place them on the seat of a rolling walker to prevent items from slipping off while transporting, or under kitchen chair cushions to lessen the chances of them slipping off.

  ▸ Use a small piece as a gripper to open bottles.

  ▸ Wrap it around a slippery grab bar to improve the grip.

  ▸ Cover the edges of hangers to secure slippery shirts or pants.

  ▸ Cut them into rectangles to create nonslip place mats.

+ Use the seat of a wheeled walker (e.g., Rollator, Medline) as a rolling cart to transport items.

+ Use a folding shopping cart to get laundry from one part of the house to another on the same floor. This also works great to transport items out to the car or around the property.

+ Smartphone cameras can help immeasurably with memory and organizing:

  ▸ Take a screen shot of their ICE (in case of emergency) information and use that as the home screen on their smartphone. It can then be easily accessed without having to unlock the phone should they be hurt and unable to communicate. They can also download an ICE page to use as their locked screen wallpaper.

  ▸ When leaving the car in a parking garage, take a picture of the floor number and space section to help find the car upon return.

  ▸ When parking in an outside lot, look around for a visual cue to help remember where the car is (a streetlamp, sign, etc.).

  ▸ Take a photo of their driver's license and passport and place them in a secure wallet app on their phone.

- Encourage them to take photos for other handy reasons:
  - Have an updated photo of their pet with her ID tags should she go missing.
  - Line up and photograph all medication bottles, one at a time, to create a visual medication list that can be taken to doctor's appointments. It is much easier than needing to create a written list each time. If they discontinue a medication or change its dosing, simply delete the old picture and take a new one.
  - Lastly, take pictures of the contents of the refrigerator and pantry. Refer to these when grocery shopping as reminders of what mom needs to buy.

Part 2

Organize—Ups and Downs

CHAPTER 9

Do Mom and Dad Need Help?

If mom and dad had their druthers, they'd continue to live in the home where they created so many memories and where they feel most comfortable. They would be among the nearly 90 percent of adults 65 and older who, according to AARP, desire to stay in their current home and community as they age.[1] And yet, in my experience, they rarely ask for help, especially the type of assistance that would go far toward keeping them safe and comfortable at home. I wish I had a dollar for every time "I'm fine" was the answer to the kids asking "How are you doing?" and "Do you need anything?"

Rather than ask, especially over a phone call from afar, you need to channel your inner Sherlock Holmes and go on a fact-finding mission. This begins with an in-person visit to their home, where the sleuthing commences. And not just one visit. Remember, though, that we all let our houses get out of hand at times, especially when overwhelmed with our many responsibilities. So if a few things are out of place, don't panic. It is a *pattern* of neglect you are looking for over a period of time that may raise a red flag, alerting you to things that need to be pursued further.

So, let's begin our sleuthing . . .

The Exterior

With your parent, walk around the outside of the house with a fresh set of eyes. Make believe you have not been there before. Look for signs that they are not keeping up with maintenance or are having difficulty managing their everyday activities. Depending on the season, check to see that all walkways and driveways are in good condition and cleared of any potential tripping hazards. Look to see if gardens and backyard sitting areas appear to be groomed and not overrun with weeds and debris. Note the condition of the roof and siding on the house, and look for signs of pest intrusion such as bird droppings or insect nests.

If there is a garage, note if it has been cleaned and swept out recently and if the path from the car to the driveway or into the house is clear and remains easy to navigate. How do the garage door and door frames look? My nana Betty was known for scraping her car against the door frame. Speaking of the car, look on all sides for dents and scrapes, an indication their driving skills may be declining.

Ask how they are doing with getting the mail and newspaper. For many of my patients this is a problem, as the newspaper often is thrown randomly toward the front of the house and ends up in the bushes or at the bottom of the steps. (See chapter 1 for suggestions how to handle this.) If they are successful retrieving their mail, it's often a good indicator of how they are doing in general, especially if the mailbox is at the end of the driveway or, as it was for a past patient of mine, literally down the block and around the corner in a bank of mailboxes.

Entrances and Exits

Watch closely as mom and dad walk into the house. Make a mental note of the answers to the following:

- If they are lucky enough to not have any steps to negotiate, can they easily get in?
- If there are steps involved, do they hold on to available railings?
- If there are no railings, do they sway at all when walking up the steps?
- Can they walk across the doormat safely?
- Can they easily put their key in the lock, grasp the doorknob, and push open the door without struggling?

Ask them which door they use most often. A side or back door leading directly into the garage or out to the driveway probably makes the most sense, as it is usually protected from the elements and most likely will get them closest to the car. I had a patient report that she went out her front door (no rails), down the front sidewalk, around to the driveway, and in a side door of her garage to get to her car . . . yet the garage was directly off the kitchen through a hallway in the back of her house! Why didn't she use the door off the kitchen? She admitted that the back hall had become a catchall for boxes and other stuff blocking the path. One decluttering project later, she could get access to her garage with increased ease.

General Living Areas

Sit down with mom and dad in the living room or den. Watch how they get on and off various pieces of furniture. Do they "plop" down into a chair with no control, landing hard on their back and butt? Do they need several tries to stand up, sometimes losing their balance before finally rising off the couch? If so, chapter 3 discusses adaptations to make the furniture easier to access.

As also noted in chapter 3, take a fresh look at the placement of the furniture to ensure that its configuration best reduces obstacles in their pathway. The most common issue I see is that coffee tables are too close to the couch, making access to the couch more difficult.

Have they been able to keep up maintenance of the floors? Wood or tile needs to be clean but not slick, and carpet and large area rugs need to be monitored for fraying and curling at the edges. Stains on the carpet may indicate they are spilling things during transport, which could be due to weakness or tremors in the upper extremities. Watch how they walk around on these floors, especially if using a cane or walker, and observe if they maintain good balance and their gait seems stable.

Is the television blasting so loud you hear it as soon as you enter the house or, as the case was with my father-in-law, as soon as you get off the elevator on the floor to his apartment? This is a potential sign of hearing loss, as is loud talking and appearing as if they are trying to read your lips.

The Kitchen

A good place to start on your sleuthing expedition in the kitchen is the refrigerator. Overall, is it clean with no bad odors? Is there plenty of food that is not spoiled? Is there a sufficient amount of fresh fruits and vegetables and not too much processed food? Is the freezer stocked with homemade food as opposed to high-sodium frozen dinners?

Check out the condition of the pots and pans. If they are burned on the bottom, it may indicate they are having some difficulty managing the cooking.

Look inside the oven and microwave to be sure they are fairly clean, with no evidence of caked-on food. I find that many of my patients no longer use their oven because pans are too heavy to lift or low vision is making it too challenging to discern which knob is for what. Toaster ovens and microwaves are often much easier to handle, especially if their location is easily accessible, as noted in chapter 4.

Determine if they seem to be losing or gaining weight, as this could indicate difficulty cooking or obtaining healthy food. Are cabinets in good order and not overflowing with junk food? Can they easily reach the items they need to prepare their food?

Besides burned pots or pans, look for signs of burns on their body. This could indicate problems transporting food from the stove, microwave, or toaster oven to the kitchen table or to the den or family room, where many of my patients prefer to eat so they can also watch the TV. Purchasing a small TV for the kitchen might alleviate this issue.

When I do an evaluation of my patients' ability to safely navigate in the kitchen, I ask them to show me how they reach the needed items they use on a regular basis. If mom or dad has favorite pots, pans, dishes, or glassware, be sure these are easily reached. Consider re-arranging items in the cabinets to ensure easier access. Chapter 4 explains decluttering and optimizing placement of items in the kitchen.

If mom or dad is not eating the foods you know they always loved, this may be a sign that they are having trouble in the kitchen. Excuses for why they no longer make their signature dish could be a sign of trouble. My friend's mother was famous for her Christmas cookies, having learned from her mother and carried on a tradition of making beautiful and delicious creations for over fifty years. Two years ago, my friend noted that the cookies were not the same taste, texture, or quality. Last year his mom confessed she could not make them anymore because she couldn't see to measure the ingredients and the batter was too difficult to mix.

The Bedroom

If the bedroom is upstairs, watch how they navigate the staircase getting there. Explore where they are actually sleeping every night. Some will end up on the couch or a recliner in the living room because they can no longer safely climb the stairs. Sometimes they'll prefer their lift chair over their bed, as noted in chapter 3, due to breathing issues that are often caused by congestive heart failure (CHF) or chronic obstructive pulmonary disease (COPD).

If possible, watch mom or dad get in and out of bed. This is where many falls occur, often due to the height of the bed, which in the past may not have been an issue. Chapter 5 explains the many ways to modify the bed to make it safer and easier to access.

Do you notice a urine smell in the bed? This is a sign of incontinence. Check to see if they have adult diapers in the bathroom and if there seems to be an excess of sheets and linens in the laundry, all signs of potential incontinence issues.

Look to see if they can easily access items on the nightstand from the bed without having to lean or reach too far. These should include a phone, flashlight, glasses and reading material if they read in bed, and the light/lamp switch.

Dirty laundry piling up may be indicative of difficulty getting to the washer and dryer.

Observe how mom and dad are dressing. If dad always wore button-down shirts and slacks and lately he has been wearing sweatpants and

T-shirts, he may have voluntarily adopted a more casual lifestyle, or he may be having trouble manipulating the buttons and zippers on the clothing he would rather be wearing.

In general, look for bruises that may denote they have been bumping into things. Increased pain or stiffness in their joints will likely impact their ability to get around the house.

The Bathroom

Do you notice any body odors when you're with mom or dad? This could be a sign of an incontinence issue or the inability to bathe thoroughly or on a regular basis. Many of my patients are afraid to get into the tub or shower. That is where they fear falling the most, and with good reason. Combine water with innately slippery surfaces and add thresholds to get over, and you are creating a scary senior scenario. They quietly morph into sponge bathers. If they are alone and the tub is tough to get into, a good daily sponge bath can do the trick. But often with the right modifications and some training, they can get safely in and out of the tub or shower and enjoy the hot water pouring on them. They will also be able to more easily reach all of their nooks and crannies to achieve complete cleanliness.

Mouth odors can be indicative of many health conditions, or they simply may have difficulty standing in front of the sink long enough to complete adequate oral hygiene. Along this line, if dad is sporting a scruffy beard, he might be going for the rugged look or it may be because he is struggling with the razor.

Around the House

Take a look at where they keep the mail. Does it appear to be fairly organized, or are there unpaid bills and statements piling up. Walk by the phone/answering machine and note whether it is blinking, indicating un-retrieved messages.

Where do mom and dad keep their pills? Most of my patients keep theirs on the kitchen counter or table. It is imperative that they are able

to manage their medications on their own. Inspect the prescription bottles to see if the medications are up to date. If you are concerned that they may not be taking their pills as directed, count the contents and compare that to the date the prescription was filled. Since taking medications seems to increase as we age, I couldn't resist adding a picture of one of my patient's kitchen table with the pills for her and her husband organized for the week. As you can see, this can become a full-time job!

If they seem to be overwhelmed with managing the bills, the pills, and the general household maintenance, you may need to probe deeper for cognitive issues. We all forget things. I cannot remember names to save my life, nor what I had for breakfast. If I don't write things down and keep a continuous to-do list, and if my walls and car dashboard weren't peppered with Post-it notes, I would be lost. Behaviors to be concerned with include getting lost driving home, not recognizing familiar objects, or displaying unsafe behaviors such as leaving the stove or oven on. Losing their keys? Welcome to my world. Finding the keys in the refrigerator? Could be trouble.

Does their behavior and temperament seem status quo? Do you notice increased talk of feeling hopeless or depressed? Are they more argumentative than usual? Do they seem paranoid? If their behavior is markedly different from usual, you may want to prod them into a visit with their primary physician.

Many think that changes in cognition and behavior are a sign that dementia is starting to rear its ugly head. These changed conditions could in fact be caused by many other medical issues, such as cancer, cardiac disease, head injuries, strokes, or systemic infections. Also, mismanaging their medications or abusing alcohol or drugs could result in cognitive or behavioral changes. Finally, deficits in sensory input such as hearing, vision, or touch could cause confusion or irritability.

Getting Out of the House

Research into the effects of social isolation on the elderly points to the fact that the more contacts and opportunities for interacting with friends and community, the better the chance of successfully aging in place.[2]

Talk to your parents about their social calendar. Are they involved in any clubs or community organizations? Do they have friends with whom they still socialize? Are they participating in physical or sporting activities?

If you live near your parents, it is easier to determine if they get out and still have a social network. Hopefully, at the very least, they are getting out with you and the rest of your supportive family. For those caregiving from afar, you may need to get in touch with their friends or check with neighbors or their faith community to establish whether they are out and about.

Here's a final bit of advice: Throughout this book I've mentioned behaviors that our parents may have stopped exhibiting, such as showering regularly, using the oven, sleeping in bed, and eating at the table. As a therapist, I initially wanted to "fix" these sorts of things. I've learned in many cases, though, that the "new normal" might just be this eventual, gradual decline of performing these activities. If they have successfully adapted to the loss of being able to do it "the old way," then there are no worries. You will have more success effecting change if you carefully pick your battles.

CHAPTER 10

You Finished the Walk, Now Have the Talk

It may be hard to initiate a discussion with your parents concerning your feelings about their ability to continue to live safely in their home. This topic is often fraught with emotions: fear, defensiveness, anger, and denial.

As an expert in the field of geriatric rehabilitation and aging in place, my phone rings several times a week with a friend, family member, or acquaintance asking for my advice about their parents. "Mom is getting weaker and toddling around the house. She is a fall waiting to happen." "Poppy fell getting into the shower and broke his hip and only has one week left in rehab before he comes home." "Dad can't get up from his recliner without mom literally pulling on him with all of her strength, and we are worried she will get hurt."

These are families on the verge of, or in the midst of, a crisis.

I cannot emphasize enough that one way to avoid, or at least minimize, this overwhelming stress is to have a plan in effect way before a crisis occurs.

We tend to be complacent as long as everyone is functioning at a good level. No one thinks they will get sick until they get sick, and you can't anticipate everything. But you can see problems coming and head them off at the pass by having "the talk" while things are status quo so plans can be established. Don't wait until mom needs a knee replacement and you realize she will not be able to get up to her bedroom and shower for eight weeks. If dad has an unexpected heart attack, it will preclude him from doing the many heavy home-maintenance chores he has done for years. What do you do then? You may not prevent a crisis, but you can make dealing with it that much easier.

Here's my advice on the subject. After all of these years, you know your family dynamics and how to approach your mom and dad about a touchy subject. The biggest stumbling block I see with families is not what should be said but the fact they don't say it. Getting the conversation started may not be easy, but it will hopefully make it possible for your parents to age safely at home. It doesn't matter what tack you take—just do it. Think of this conversation in a positive way, about how you and your parents can work together to keep them in their own home. The good news is you are not talking about exploring assisted living or nursing homes. The talk is, of course, spurred by your concern, but it's not just about feelings. It is a presentation of your findings from the research you conducted in chapter 9 with a goal to analyze potential trouble spots and make a plan to fix them.

The Family Caregiver Alliance has a wonderful tip sheet on how to hold a family meeting.[1] It suggests an agenda that includes such topics as health issues, daily caregiving needs, financial concerns, and more. It also offers suggestions for where the meeting should take place, who should run it, and who should be in attendance. It concludes with possible challenges to prepare for. Remember that one meeting is just the beginning of an ongoing, ever-changing scenario involving complex issues.

So call a family meeting. It's time to get organized.

CHAPTER 11

Form the Team and Prepare to Care

Part 1 of this book focused on how to evaluate, modify, declutter, and organize mom and dad's house. From my perspective, those are the most important physical aspects of ensuring their ability to successfully age in place. This perspective is based on the concept that activities will be easier to accomplish if "environmental press" (the degree to which the environment presents challenges, making it harder to function in that environment) is reduced.[1]

But there is more.

If the appropriate modifications have been made and all agree that the house has now been deemed manageable and safe, it is important to not fall into the trap of complacency. In addition to creating an ideal environment to ensure success, it is integral to monitor your parents' health and facilitate their engagement with friends and community. You've heard the saying "it takes a village"? It does.

I have worked with geriatric patients for over thirty-seven years, the last thirteen in the home care arena. My role as an occupational therapist puts me right in the trenches, as I end up in their house within days of them returning home from the hospital or rehab facility. The patients who most successfully recover and safely continue on at home have a strong and organized support system. The kids are on the same page and have arranged a thorough coverage plan for mom and dad. Tasks that can be tackled well ahead of a crisis have been completed. What type of tasks are we talking about?

Building the Team

Creating a team to assist with your parents is the first and one of the most essential tasks. Trying to do everything yourself may lead to burnout and problems with your own physical and mental health. Reach out and form a larger network of friends, family, and community resources that can assume various responsibilities.

Start with the Family

The first level of help ordinarily includes siblings and other immediate family members. In an ideal world the siblings would be available and eager to help, but unfortunately this is not always the case. A great resource for family caregivers that I referenced in chapter 10 is the Family Caregiver Alliance,[2] which can provide helpful strategies on getting family members to kick in when it comes to caring for mom and dad.

Many of the overwhelmed caregivers I work with admit they haven't picked up the phone and asked for help. They believe their family members should recognize on their own how much they have taken on and take the initiative to offer help. In reality, we all get caught up in our own lives and responsibilities and may be unaware of the burden on the primary caregiver. Receiving a call with a specific request for help can be the impetus for spurring family members to get involved.

Siblings who live the closest often become the "team leader" with the most to do. However, team members do not have to live close by or have large blocks of time available in order to help. The brother who lives far away could be responsible for paying all the bills and offering other types of financial assistance online. The sister who works full-time could set up electronic calendars and organize all of the medical appointments at her convenience. Grandchildren are often an overlooked commodity. Teenagers can provide companionship, personal care, and light household maintenance. If all else fails and the family can't seem to be united in a coordinated effort, consideration could be given to sitting with a neutral counselor to facilitate communication and guide everyone toward a cooperative care plan.

Look Outside the Box

If you don't have siblings to help, your parents may be able to identify potential team members you have not considered. They may have nieces and nephews available to help, if asked. Your parents' friends and neighbors may be able to offer invaluable assistance. Helpful neighbors can be your eyes and ears. Consider giving them a spare key to the house in case mom gets locked out or if someone needs to gain access to check on things. Churches, synagogues, and other faith communities may be worth contacting, too—they often have formal committees in place to provide outreach to their senior congregants.

Creating a help network, especially if you live a distance from mom and dad, is critical. Help mom and dad create an emergency contact plan with family, neighbors, and anyone else you've recruited that details who to call and in which order when help is needed short of 911. I recommend that my patients write down all their emergency contacts with phone numbers on large index cards and place a card by every phone in the house and on the refrigerator. It is hard to remember this info in an emergency.

Don't forget to add a handyman to the care team. Whether a family member, friend, or a professional contractor, make sure they know what they are doing. While adding a banister to a staircase may be simple, installing a grab bar into a tile shower is complicated. Having someone "on call" who has already been vetted and has a reputation for good work will alleviate stress when a modification is needed.

If you are truly alone and you cannot find anyone to join the team, look into hiring a geriatric care manager. Geriatric care managers provide advice and coordination of care for seniors and their families and are particularly helpful when families are geographically separated. Check out the Aging Life Care Association website to find a professional near your parent and for more information.[3]

Prepare to Care

Getting a handle on your aging parents' health is going to be one of your biggest and most time-consuming tasks. All the appointments, medications, and treatments can become overwhelming if you don't stay organized and proactive.

Educate Yourself about Their Diagnosis

Knowledge is power, and the more you know the more you will understand what to expect.

Learning as much as you can about your loved ones' physical health is a good place to start. The internet offers an unlimited amount of information on any and all diagnoses. Discerning what is important, factual, and reliable, however, can be a challenge. For starters, I recommend beginning your research by going to the official association for the disease or condition in question. If dad is showing early signs of dementia, for example, you can learn a great deal from the Alzheimer's Association website.[4]

Just as professional caregivers do, you can receive caregiving training or gain fresh knowledge through online resources or community organizations. To be an effective advocate for your parents, you should update yourself on specific conditions and ailments, how to care for people with physical or mental disabilities, legal and financial issues, and end-of-life issues. Videos are available for every situation, such as how to manage a wheelchair when transferring people on and off of various surfaces to setting up a room in the house for hospice care.

Understand Their Health Insurance Plan

A critical aspect of caring for your aging parents is understanding their available health and medical insurance benefits and how best to use them.

Sometimes the hardest thing to do is find the benefits book or membership information packet that outlines their coverage plan. Once you do, invest an hour and read through it. Some are harder to understand than others. If there are parts you don't understand, high-light them so you can call a representative and get clarification. It is important that you familiarize yourself with all benefits offered.

Some of the key points to look for include:

+ How does the coverage work?

+ What are the deductibles and the amount of co-pays?

+ When are prior authorizations required?

+ Are their doctors and preferred hospitals covered by the plan?

+ Have plan benefits changed from the preceding year?

+ What is their medication coverage?

Create a Coverage Plan for the Kids and Others

Much has been written about the "Sandwich Generation"—caregivers who are squeezed between simultaneously caring for children and an elder family member. As people live longer, this can become a multi-generational situation as we simultaneously care for a combination of children, grandchildren, parents, and grandparents—not to mention ourselves and our spouses. No one can do it all. One trick to success is to organize coverage for the various people for whom you are responsible.

One issue people fail to consider in advance is determining who will watch the kids if we are called upon for a parental emergency. Mom takes a fall and the ambulance is on its way and it's your turn for carpool in an hour. Having a "kid coverage" plan lined up alleviates the stress when being unexpectedly pulled in all directions. Write down all necessary information about your child so it will be available to provide to a helper at a moment's notice. This should include their daily routine or schedule, along with the names of teachers, babysitters, and camp counselors dur-ing the summer season, along with their appropriate contact informa-tion. Details like the names of bus drivers, bus schedules, and school nurses are important to pass on to your designee if you are called away.

You may also want to prepare a sheet for after-school activity contacts, such as piano teachers and coaches. Also, fill out a medical release on your kids should someone have to provide them emergency medical care. Research "child medical release form" for many options.

Besides mom and dad, you may be responsible for grandma or aunt Muriel. Have pertinent information on that person readily available should you need to share it with an interim helper while you are dealing with your parents.

Educate Yourself about Community Supports

Your parents' local or state Area Agency on Aging will be able to offer a full list of agencies that provide various services. Familiarize yourself with local home care offerings, including in-home aide services, respite and senior centers, adult day services, and dementia programs so that you are prepared should the need arise to utilize any of these support programs. Other resources for transportation, home-delivered meals, and legal and financial assistance are also available.

Document an Emergency Plan

Think of potential emergencies that might arise and generate a contingency plan. Actually role-play with your parent. What would they do if, for example, they took a fall? What steps should they take to get help? Who should they call first?

Create two identical "health care notebooks" (one for them and one to keep at your house) with sections for doctors who treat them, along with detailed contact information (don't forget after hours/emergency phone numbers), their medical history, a medication list with dosages and frequency of use, copies of test results and blood work, and insurance information. (See "What May Be Included in the Health Care Notebook" in part 3 for more detailed information.) This should be placed in a "grab and go" location that everyone should know about. Keep this updated.

One of the outcomes you want to achieve when having "the talk" with your parents is to determine what they would want done for them in a medical emergency. Encourage them to fill out advance directives, including a health care proxy and living will, and have them properly notarized. Copies should be distributed to their primary doctor, lawyer, and chosen health care agent.

Long-Distance Caregiving

Being organized includes maintaining twenty-four-hour accessibility to your loved one, whether they live around the corner or thousands of miles away. In an emergency, minutes could make the difference between life and death. How can this be accomplished if you live far away?

You and your parent should create an emergency list with phone numbers for first responders (ambulance, fire, and police), plus phone numbers and addresses for local hospitals (in case you have to pop it into your GPS and get on the road fast). Besides ensuring that family, friends, and your parents' neighbors have that list, you must keep it available for yourself at all times (don't forget to have a copy at work or in your car if you're traveling). And remember, the list will only remain effective if its information is kept up to date.

Schedule your parents' doctor's appointments to coincide with your visits so you can meet and become familiar with the practitioners and their staff. Be sure mom and dad list your name as a person who should be considered privy to their medical information when they are filling out HIPAA (Health Insurance Portability and Accountability Act) forms. While you may be pacing in the airport trying to get a flight out and simultaneously trying to find out how dad is doing, without your inclusion on the HIPAA forms, the medical staff is legally prohibited from discussing your father's situation with you. Have them check with their various doctors' offices to ensure all HIPAA forms are up to date, and, as they deem appropriate, include the names of any other members of their care team who should be privy to their medical information.

One of the best ways to keep an eye on someone who lives far away is to create some type of a check-in system. Create a schedule, with the help of family and friends so that someone is calling and checking on mom or dad each day. Another option is to hire a telephone reassurance service to make daily calls to check on mom or dad's well-being. With these services, if there is no contact after a few attempts, they will call designated people, based on a priority list you provided, until they reach someone who can check in on the folks. If they get no response after going down the call list, they will contact emergency responders. Search "phone check-in systems for seniors" on the web and you will find many options with various price ranges. Most charge by the month.

The employees of the US Postal Service provide an innovative outreach system called the Carrier Alert Program. Often the letter carrier is the only person who is at the senior's home almost every day. If a person wants to participate, a local social service agency notifies the local post office and a sticker is placed inside the mailbox. If the mail starts to accumulate, or something seems out of place such as no tracks in the snow, pets barking or crying, or curtains never being open, the letter carrier notifies the appropriate people. To find out if there is such a program in place where your parent lives, contact the National Association of Letter Carriers (NALC) or the local post office.[5]

Here are some more organizing tips to make long-distance caregiving easier:

+ Create an emergency travel plan for yourself. Could you get to your parents at a moment's notice? List transportation information to facilitate your traveling, such as phone numbers and schedules for planes, trains, and buses. Have a route mapped out if you're within driving distance. Have rental car information already researched. Be sure your passport is up to date if applicable.

+ Obtain an updated copy of your parents' community telephone directory, both white and yellow pages. This will list senior services that you can access as different needs arise. You may need to create your own list from online resources.

+ To ensure twenty-four-hour access to your loved one's property, make duplicate keys, plastic access cards, and electronic openers, and know the combinations to any locks and keypads. Label keys with your parents' name (but not their address in case a key should become misplaced), and be sure to distribute to designated neighbors and friends.

+ If your parent has voice mail on the phone and email on the computer, learn their access codes and passwords so you can retrieve messages.

+ Know all of their passwords for important online sites and bank accounts so you can monitor their business dealings should they became unable to do so on their own.

+ Obtain or update power of attorney paperwork. If your parent is suddenly incapacitated, you will need this to deal with their banks, credit card companies, medical providers, and the like.

CHAPTER 12

Organize and Assign the Tasks— Share the Care

In chapters 1 through 8, you completed a walk-through of the house and learned tips for modifying and decluttering to make it safer and more manageable. In chapters 9 through 11, you learned the foundation for forming a caregiving team that will augment the support mom and dad will need to successfully stay in their home. To complete the formation of your plan to help them continue to thrive at home, the occupational therapist in me suggests you evaluate mom and dad's abilities to live independently by observing their ability to complete activities of daily living (ADLs) and instrumental activities of daily living (IADLs). Based on the results of your ADL and IADL evaluation, determine how best to share their care. That is the focus of this chapter.

As noted in the introduction, ADLs consist of eating, personal hygiene, dressing, toileting, and transferring from surface to surface. IADLs include transportation, maintaining finances, home maintenance, using the phone, and managing medications.

No one person can fulfill all your parents' needs in these areas. Rather, by listing all of them and dividing the responsibility, they can become manageable. For example, mom has a doctor's appointment next week and you can't leave work for the millionth time. You have a cousin who is retired and has said, "Let me know if you ever need me to help." For her, taking your mom to the doctors for two hours is neither an imposition nor a long-term commitment, but it can take the stress off of you about taking time off from work yet again. Successful caregiving takes organization and the moxie to ask for backup. Share the care!

After you have generated a list of needs, determine who will be in charge of each one. Simply draw a line down the middle of a piece of paper and list on the left side all the areas where they need help. Next to each need put the name, availability, and contact information for the person in charge. You can also create a document on your computer, such as an Excel spreadsheet, that you can share with everyone online.

Everyday Tasks

It's time again for more meetings as you explore with your parents how they are functioning in these areas. The following are the areas of daily life I've found most troublesome for my patients. Bathing and dressing are considered ADLs; meal preparation and home maintenance are IADLs.

Bathing

One area of significant concern, even after I discharge a patient, is their trepidation about getting into the tub or shower on their own. Once I have ascertained that they have the optimum setup for safety, which always includes grab bars and may include some seats and other equipment, I make the following suggestion: When they are about to get into the shower or tub, they should call a designated family member or friend and simply tell them they are getting in. Afterward, call again as soon as they are safely out. If for some reason after twenty minutes that second call doesn't come, it's time to activate whatever plan is in place to respond to the situation. It's kind of like a free personal emergency response system for bathing. This is a good example of a need that can be assigned to anyone on the list, near or far, as long as they have a phone.

Dressing

Deciding what to wear, especially during changing weather conditions, can sometimes be difficult for mom or dad. Have someone take on the task of helping to choose and lay out a week's worth of outfits, perhaps on the bed in another room or placed together on hangers that can be easily reached.

Food and Meal Preparation

As discussed in chapter 9, your parents may be hesitant to accept that managing meals has become overwhelming. After all, it was their job to feed their kids nourishing meals as they were growing up, and to admit they can't cook anymore is a large defeat. Noticing weight loss or hearing them say they have no appetite may be a by-product of a medical problem. However, if they seem otherwise healthy, you need to delve deeper to see if the mere thought of shopping for, prepping, and cooking a meal has become too much to handle.

Some options to help include researching stores that deliver groceries; ordering from one of several online companies that deliver all of the fresh ingredients needed to make several days' worth of meals; and signing them up for home-delivered meals. Research "meal delivery" to explore the many available options.

Preparing meals is certainly a good addition to the needs list, and it's helpful to assign somebody to oversee the preparation and delivery. Organizing neighbors, friends, and relatives to make a few meals will quickly fill the freezer, and before you know it you will have gathered a month's worth of food.

Home Maintenance

This is an area where family and friends can be very helpful. Look at the list of needs generated from your walk-through of the house and grounds. Grandchildren are good candidates to enlist for mowing or snow removal. If they have a neighbor who is on the same trash-removal schedule, perhaps when they take their own cart down to the curb they could grab mom's cart also and then bring it back up the next day. Neighbors are also handy for bringing the mail up if the mailbox is not attached to the house.

Medication Management

The more mom and dad know about the medications they are taking, the better the chances of a successful outcome. Here are some ways you can help them.

Help Them to Understand Their Pills

We often end a doctor's appointment with new prescriptions in hand. Before leaving, make sure mom or dad can read the prescription. If they can't, it might be difficult for the pharmacist too, despite their practice in deciphering doctors' handwriting. Some common prescription abbreviations include "po" (by mouth), "qd" (daily), "bid" (twice a day), "tid" (three times a day), "qid" (four times a day), "hs" (at night), and "prn" (as needed). To ensure safety and effectiveness, it is important to understand the specifics about each medication they take. This includes knowing what is being prescribed, what it does, when to take it, and how long before it "starts to work."

The US Food and Drug Administration (FDA) advises that all medications carry some risk of harmful reactions. If you have ever read the insert listing possible side effects that accompanies your prescription, you may wonder whether the risks outweigh the benefits. Even over-the-counter common cold remedies list side effects that can sound ominous. Regardless, we are in charge of correctly using both prescribed and over-the-counter medications. Mom and dad need to understand what possible side effects are likely and what monitoring may need to be done, such as periodic blood work. They should note any side effects in their health care notebook, specifically describing what happened, when, and how long it lasted. They may need a little nudging to record these details in a timely fashion and to report it to their doctor.

Here are some additional tips to help them organize and manage their medications:

+ Know the names of medications, both the brand name (e.g., Motrin, Tylenol) and the generic name (e.g., ibuprofen, acetaminophen).

+ Know what the pills look like. Taking photos of each medicine, printing them out, and attaching them to index cards along with the medication name can help everyone learn and differentiate the pills. It's sort of like flash cards for medicine. Generic prescription pills can come in different shapes, colors, and sizes, so be sure to update these cards as needed.

+ Read and understand all of the directions on the medication container.

+ Know what to do if they skip a dose.

Help Them Organize and Remember to Take Their Pills

Not taking prescribed medication can result in serious consequences. Research indicates that people are compliant with their prescriptions only 50 percent of the time.[1] Why don't people take their medicine? Some do not understand directions on how to take it, some begin to feel better and stop, and many simply forget. Some of my patients describe managing medications, especially if it's for themselves and their "other half," as a full-time job.

If mom and dad are on multiple medications, keeping their information organized can be overwhelming. One simple solution is to create a chart with the following information:

+ the brand name and generic name of the drug

+ the dosage/strength of the pill

+ how many times per day they should take it and when

+ the condition for which they are taking the specific medication

+ any special directions (e.g., take with or without food; avoid driving)

This chart should include prescription drugs, over-the-counter medications, nutritional supplements, and vitamins. Remind them to always keep the chart updated and bring it with them to all doctor appointments.

There are numerous medication-organizing systems to help prompt people to take their pills. The most common is a pillbox with individual compartments labeled by the day. Some are further divided into compartments for morning, noon, and evening. With one glance you can see what needs to be taken when, or if a dose has been missed.

Electronic pillboxes offer a variety of programmable alarms, including chimes, beeps, and even voices that say "take your pills." Alarm clocks and pagers can help prompt when it is time to take their pills. There are watch-like reminder alarms that sound or vibrate at designated times and others with LED readouts with the name of the pills and other relevant information. Of course, "there's an app for that," too. Check out the app store on your smartphone for abundant medication reminder offerings.

Electronic pill dispensers not only remind the user to take their pills, they also dispense the correctly programmed dose. This is an excellent option when the caregiver cannot be on site and the patient has memory impairments. These dispensers can be programmed up to thirty days in advance, provide different types of reminders (voice, text, and blinking lights), and eventually will call the caregiver if the medications are not taken on time. Note that power outages often require these devices to be reset, so periodically ask mom how the dispenser is working.

One patient of mine, who kept her preset pillbox on the kitchen table, would get settled into bed at night and realize she had not taken her evening pills. I took a large, brightly colored index card, folded it in half so it would stand, wrote "take your pills" on it with a dark marker, and placed it on her night table. This low-tech solution simply created a visual prompt in a specific location that served as an effective reminder. Another option is to leave a separate pillbox for evening medication next to the bed, along with a spill-proof water bottle.

It is so important that mom and dad take their pills correctly and on time. Compliance can impact their ability to continue to live independently and safely in their home. To ensure they can continue to do so, here are some tips:

+ Inquire if the medication can be dosed in longer-acting pills to avoid having to take multiple smaller doses during the day.

+ According to AARP, memory is based on effectively putting new information into your mind. When starting a new medication, they recommend that the patient repeat the instructions five to ten times. Read them, say them out loud, sing them—do whatever it takes to internalize the information.[2]

+ Connect pill taking with an established routine to serve as a visual reminder. Place the medications near the coffee maker, where they hang their keys, or on the night table if taking pills before bed is prescribed.

+ Ask the pharmacist to prepare medications in non-childproof bottles for easier opening. These bottles need to be secured or monitored when grandchildren are present.

+ Many of my patients flip the cover over on the bottles and screw them on upside down for easier opening.

+ Use a thick permanent marker to write the name of the medication and the dose on the label.

Transportation

Driving provides real freedom and independence, which our parents are understandably reluctant to give up despite declines in vision, hearing, strength, mobility, and perhaps memory. It's important to monitor their driving skills and be aware of signs that it may be time to find alternative means of transportation for them.

Safe Driving for Mom and Dad

One day my 80-year-old nana pulled her car out of a side road, overshot the median, and drove down the wrong side of a four-lane divided highway. Fortunately, she and the other unsuspecting drivers on the road that day lived to tell about it. She said she knew she was in trouble when everyone else seemed to be going the wrong way. This was a clearcut sign that it was time to limit her driving, if not stop it altogether. More often, the warning signs are more subtle.

The ability to drive safely is a matter of function, not age. The standard measure is based on visual acuity—how much detail they see. For example, diminished contrast sensitivity, such as the ability to distinguish a black car or a pedestrian at night, is the cause of many problems. As we age, various medical conditions may impact driving by causing weakness, loss of flexibility, stiff joints, and cognitive impairments such as difficulty concentrating and slowing of reaction time. Medications may also cause drowsiness and affect mental functioning.

How do you know when it's time for mom and dad to limit or stop driving? Observe or ask if they are:

+ noticing more dents and scrapes on the car, or needing to swerve to avoid close calls. (Nana had taken out the garage door at her apartment several weeks before the wrong-way driving incident.)

+ feeling nervous about driving, or realizing that others won't drive with them.

+ having more difficulty merging onto highways, changing lanes, or getting through intersections or rotaries.

+ weaving in and out of driving lanes.

+ getting honked at more frequently.

+ feeling like cars or pedestrians come "out of nowhere."

+ noticing slower reaction time when braking or moving from the gas to the brake.

+ having difficulty turning or backing up due to stiffness in their neck, arms, or torso.

+ forgetting where they are going, or getting confused with directions.

Experiencing one or more of these warning signs doesn't automatically mean it's time to hand over the keys. Consider a classroom refresher course. Some of my occupational therapy colleagues specialize in assessing driving performance and can make recommendations for the driver and suggest modifications for the car, such as larger mirrors, pedal extenders, and easy-locking seat belts. Most importantly, start a dialogue based on the above list, and create a plan so when the time comes it is not so traumatic.

Finally, suggest the following tips to help take control of driving skills and plan ahead for a safe drive:

+ Have their vision and hearing tested annually. At certain advanced ages they may need to submit these results to the Department of Motor Vehicles in order to renew their operator's license.

+ If possible, drive only in daylight and good weather.

+ Avoid peak traffic times and busy highways.

+ Map out the route in advance.

+ Maintain fitness and flexibility.

+ Investigate tinted eyeglass lenses to increase contrast, enhance night driving, and decrease glare.

Plan Ahead Before They Stop Driving

Several programs are available to help older drivers learn to compensate for decreases in skills, and physical adaptations to cars are sometimes possible. Still, most likely there will come a day when mom and dad should no longer drive. The time is now, while they are still on the road, to create a future transportation plan.

Where to begin? Start by thinking: If the car broke down today, how would that impact their life? Make a list of everything they do that involves driving. General areas might include going to work (if still applicable) and doctor's appointments, picking up medications, grocery shopping, socializing and recreation, and attending religious services. Once the list is created, start exploring alternative methods to accomplish the designated tasks.

When making your list, consider the possible barriers to success and brainstorm some solutions. For example, if they are concerned about relying too much on family and friends, research availability of volunteer drivers through churches, synagogues, or senior centers. Cut down on the number of rides needed by scheduling several appointments on the same day or having medications or groceries delivered.

So don't wait for the day when the doctor or other family members recommend that your parent give up their keys. Start getting organized now by helping them to create a transportation plan. Here's how to go about it:

+ Make a list of phone numbers and/or web addresses for public transportation options, including buses, cabs, Uber, Lyft, or other car services.

+ Go to the website of their local bus company for maps and schedules, and cross-reference this with the destinations they frequently visit.

+ Familiarize them with the various senior-friendly features of public transportation. Most buses, for example, are equipped for wheelchair use if needed and have a "kneeling device" that lowers the first step to curb level.

+ Consider ordering medications by mail, which is convenient and often cheaper. Some pharmacies will deliver.

+ Check if their local grocery store delivers.

+ Shop on the internet or order through catalogs via the mail or phone.

+ Familiarize yourself with the offerings of your nearest Area Agency on Aging and check out other local resources that may provide transportation, meals, or respite care.

+ If they are concerned about identification, they can get a non-driver identification card from the Department of Motor Vehicles. The non-driver ID has the same personal identification information, photo, signature, and special safeguards against alterations as a normal driver's license. It just does not permit them to drive.

Finances

Here is where the computer-savvy family member comes in. Set up an online banking account with various electronic payment systems. Have Social Security and pension checks direct deposited, and arrange for automatic payment of recurring bills. If she is ready to relinquish control, have mom's bills sent to the designated helper to pay online from her account, even if the helper is thousands of miles away. She must authorize the designee to act on her behalf by signing a power of attorney.

If the designee is a trusted family member, another alternative is to create a joint bank account giving that person the ability to conduct transactions. If your parents have a safe deposit box, have your name added as someone who can access it if needed. If no one on the team is able or willing to help with finances, consider hiring a daily money manager who can go to their home once or twice a month to help them pay their bills. Visit the American Association of Daily Money Managers website to find out more information about these professionals who provide financial services to seniors.[3]

Help Them Get Their Affairs in Order

The worst-case scenario is needing to access vital information for mom or dad in a crisis situation and having no clue where anything is. They have accumulated a lifetime of information that is likely scattered in various locations both inside and outside of their home. I highly recommend to my patients that they create a detailed list, a "treasure map" if you will, of how to find their most important records, documents, and belongings so that should something happen to them, the kids aren't left scrambling to produce this information. The map will provide details or "clues" of where these vital documents live. One clue might be a simple statement like, "In the top drawer of the desk in the den is a file marked 'insurance' that contains copies of health insurance cards, life insurance policies with beneficiaries, long-term care policies, and our homeowners' and auto insurance policies." Another clue would be, "The safe deposit box is at the Bank of America branch located in Guilderland, the key is in the little red envelope in my top dresser drawer, and the box number is written on the envelope." In some instances, the clues could be purposely cryptic to safeguard the information, such as, "Access my bank online at bac.com. The user name is my last name, and the password is our wedding anniversary date."

The vital documents list (see part 3), which I fondly call "the Mother List," is a list of all the important information you need to know about mom or dad. Sit down with them and create the map to these all-important documents, and keep it updated and in a safe yet easily accessible place. It will save so much angst if you know exactly where to find these papers should you need to get your hands on them quickly.

Health Issues

As noted in chapter 11, it is very helpful for you to learn at least the basics about any medical problems mom or dad has been diagnosed with. This will allow you to speak with their medical team more intelligently and understand why certain treatment decisions are being made. You can keep an online or paper file of data in a folder created specifically for mom and dad's medical information.

Get to know your parents' medical team—the doctors, of course, but also the ancillary medical staff, including nurse practitioners and physician assistants. Try to get contact information for them, as they are the ones who may be providing treatment on a regular basis. The office staff, especially the appointment schedulers, are key personnel, and I highly suggest you befriend them early and keep in friendly touch often. They are the gatekeepers to the doctor, and if you have established a good relationship it may help when trying to quickly get mom in for an appointment.

Learn the culture of the office. How do you make appointments? How do you get test results? Can you view the results online? What do you do in an emergency, and how do you contact them during off hours?

Ensure the contact information the office has for you is always kept updated.

Be sure dad has signed HIPAA forms designating you as a person who's authorized to access his health information. Otherwise, legally they cannot discuss anything with you concerning his medical condition.

Create a Health Care Notebook

There are three basic states of health that we flow in and out of throughout our life: wellness, acute illness, and adaptation to a chronic disease (for instance, living with diabetes, heart disease, or arthritis). And throughout our life, we accumulate volumes of health-related information.

What most of us do not do is ascertain what information is most important, when that data might be useful, and how to quickly access it should the need arise. If you maintain everything in a central place, it will be much easier to find and share information when necessary. In other words, compile it and file it.

Each person has their own way of organizing information. It is important that you choose a system that works best for you so you will maintain it. For me, a large three-ring binder with tabbed dividers, pocket folders, and sheets for holding business cards is ideal. Think about your parents' situation when creating sections. Here are my suggestions:

- *Doctors.* Include information for everyone who treats them, as well as affiliated hospitals with detailed contact information. (Don't forget after-hours/emergency phone numbers.)

- *Medical History.* Includes summaries of pertinent past diagnoses, surgeries, and chronic medical conditions.

- *Test Results.* Use separate pocket folder dividers for related sets of results (e.g., one for their heart test results, one for dermatology, etc.).

- *Medications.* Update the information in this section whenever medications or dosages are changed.

- *Wellness Checkup Schedules.*

- *Insurance Information.*

If you are designing the book for someone with an acute or chronic condition, you should add two more sections:

- *Treatment Information.*

- *Home Health Services.* (See part 3 for more details.)

Start it now, before any medical crisis arises, and keep this notebook updated. Taking it with you when you accompany them to medical appointments is a great way to keep it up to date. Your parents should have the hard copy of the health care notebook, and you can either make a duplicate notebook or create a computer-based record for yourself to ensure twenty-four-hour access to information that can be easily updated.

Advance Directives

Most people don't want to think about end-of-life issues. We believe there will always be plenty of time to consider and execute these very important decisions. Yet life can change on a dime, at any age, and without warning. If your parents don't have advance health care directives, the time to think about them is now. Why? Because they need to research and understand that making these decisions is an ongoing conversation about values, priorities, and what quality of life means to them. Circumstances change, and advance planning for health care is a work in progress. No one is too young to consider this.

Advance health care directives consist of a living will, which specifies what kind of treatment they would want should they become incapacitated, and a health care proxy (i.e., health care power of attorney), which names an agent they have chosen to make medical decisions for them. Most states recognize both the proxy and the living will, but interpretations may vary, and most lawyers agree that having both documents is the most effective. Aside from the legal ramifications of advance directives, there is the emotional aspect of letting your loved ones know exactly what your wishes are.

When choosing a health care proxy, mom or dad should consider someone who will be willing and able to convey their wishes without letting their own feelings interfere. Most of my patients choose one of their children, if applicable. My advice to them is to choose someone who knows and understands them well, lives close by, will be available hopefully long into the future, and is capable of being a strong advocate for them in the face of possible conflict between family, doctors, and institutions. They should also select an alternate proxy to act as their agent should the primary proxy not be available.

Here are some organizing tips for mom and dad to help prepare and maintain advance health care directives:

+ Keep the original in a safe but accessible location, but not in a safe deposit box or place where others can't find it.

+ Give copies to their proxy, alternate proxy, doctors, clergy, family, friends, or anyone involved in their health care. Tell the proxy where the original document is located.

+ The American Bar Association Commission on Law and Aging recommends reevaluating one's wishes if any of the "five Ds" occur: reaching a new decade of life, a divorce, a serious critical diagnosis, a decline in health, or the death of a close loved one.

+ If they enter a hospital or nursing home, have the directives placed in their medical record.

+ If they wish to make changes to their directive, complete new documents and redistribute to everyone involved.

+ Advance directives do not cover avoiding cardiopulmonary resuscitation (CPR) if an ambulance (911) is called. If they do not want CPR done at home, they need a "do not resuscitate" (DNR) order that will be respected outside of a hospital. The form, called a MOLST (medical treatment orders for life-sustaining treatment), is signed by the physician as well as by the consenting patient or that patient's power of attorney. It is usually printed on pink paper and should be placed prominently in the home. Most tend to put it in an envelope and tape it to the front of the refrigerator so that it can be easily found if needed.

+ In legal matters such as these, it is best to contact your attorney for advice.

Hiring Help for Mom and Dad

Even after all of the modifications have been made and all the informal supports are in place, there may come a time when paid help in the home on a consistent basis is needed to facilitate aging in place. My experience has found that hiring a home health aide often makes the difference between nursing home placement and staying at home.

The first step in securing an aide is deciding whether to use an agency or hire privately. Each has its benefits. Referrals from trusted professionals, family, and friends are one of the best ways to find a good aide. Private, freelance, or independent caregivers can also be found in the "situations wanted" section of newspapers. Private hires are often less expensive than going through an agency, but many are not licensed and do not accept insurance. Whatever the compensation agreement, consult an accountant to understand tax and labor requirements, and follow the laws as they pertain to the contract you devise. (And that is an important point: be sure to have everything in writing so there are no misunderstandings, including such things as schedules, duties, and payment details.)

A potential negative of hiring privately is that independent contractors have generally not been subjected to a thorough vetting process or background check. It is important to conduct interviews, check references, and get a personal referral from someone you know if possible. Another issue is to ensure sufficient coverage when the aide needs to take time off. One solution is to look for private aides who have grouped together to provide cover for each other as needed. Be sure you know and approve of everyone who might be caring for your parent.

Agencies usually employ people who have been vetted and possess licenses or certifications to provide necessary services to your family member. The service providers can range from companions to certified home health aides to skilled nurses who can provide things like medication management and wound care and act as a liaison with the person's doctor. Fees for an agency are generally more than that for a private caregiver, as it also must cover the cost of mandatory employee benefits and insurance coverage. Such employees are often bondable, meaning the agency carries liability insurance for their actions. In addition to accepting private payments, agencies often accept various health insurance, long-term care insurance, and in some cases Medicaid.

People often ask me how much aide time I think they need. One way to make that determination is to analyze mom or dad's routine. Caregivers can provide everything from personal care such as dressing, bathing, and toileting to making meals, monitoring medications, and driving to appointments or errands. Ascertain if your mom needs help every time she gets up to move versus just needing monitoring for a shower or maybe help with meals, or if dad stays in bed safely for the night or is up several times a night going to the bathroom. One approach is to have a few hours of coverage in the morning to get them up, washed, and dressed and prepare their breakfast. Lunch can also be prepared and left for later on. Then someone could come back for a few hours at night to prepare dinner and help them get ready for bed.

Whether you hire privately or through an agency, get organized by getting the answers to these questions:

+ How long have they been in business?

+ If an agency, are they bonded, licensed, and insured?

+ Do they have at least three references?

+ What is their coverage policy?

+ Do they have special skills such as experience working with dementia or knowledge of how to use mechanical lifts?

+ Don't forget the human aspect. Does it feel like a good match?

+ Does your parent like and feel comfortable with the aide? Do you?

Create Command Central

No matter what shape your parent is in, from highly independent to fairly debilitated, creating a place in the home where pertinent information is contained and easily accessible is one of my favorite organizing tips. A desk in the kitchen, a table in the family room, or a large corner shelf by the back door are all examples of viable options. The point here is that everyone on the team, including your parent, will always know where to go to find all they need to know without searching.

Place a dry-erase board on the wall above the table, where fluctuating information can be updated as needed. Examples of subjects for the board include who's coming in that day (e.g., daily therapists) and who's bringing food.

On a desk or kitchen table, keep a notebook for all caregivers to write a daily entry. Each time anyone has contact with mom or dad, they should record the date and time and jot a note in the book. Whether it's a reaction to what they ate, the effect their medication

had on them, or simply their mood that day, documenting this information will create an ongoing daily log that will provide a wealth of information and chronological record of their progress. A phrase or sentence or two is sufficient, and it will eventually combine to form an accurate synopsis of their health over a period of weeks and months.

Make room on the table for the health care notebook, home care information such as exercises and therapy, and information regarding durable medical equipment in the home. Office supply stores offer attractive vertical dividers or horizontal shelves to hold the folders. There should be a master list of key players with all of their contact information.

Besides the dry-erase board, I also recommend placing a calendar on or above the table with all appointments neatly recorded. It is imperative that this single schedule of activities be kept in one place, as it can become confusing and difficult to act on if it moves to various locations.

There are many apps to help caregivers become and stay organized. Everyone on the care team can download everything they need and share information about tasks, medications, doctors, appointments, and virtually everything to keep your parent and the team organized and informed.

Conclusion

I was delighted recently to attend the one hundredth birthday party of a former patient who I kept in touch with because her wit, charm, and amazing personality made all who knew her want to continue to be in her life. Billie wanted a celebration surrounded by those who were meaningful to her, and the restaurant was packed. The crowd included her children, grandchildren, great-grandchildren, nieces, nephews, cousins, friends, neighbors, the cleaning woman, the beautician, her aide, merchants from shops she frequented, fellow parishioners, and even the archdeacon of the diocese. Several of her doctors were there, as well as her favorite occupational, physical, and mobility therapists. It was an amazing tribute.

Billie has used this circle of support to help fulfill her dream of aging in place.

She lives alone in a ranch home in upstate New York. For all intents and purposes she is blind, with only a smidge of peripheral vision that, with the right light and huge magnification, allows her to enjoy glimpses of her great-grandchildren. With the help of a private aide a few hours a day and the above-mentioned circle of support, she manages to function independently and remain an active, contributing member of her community.

Although the need for this book had been percolating in my mind for years, Billie became the impetus to get it done. Her family is far away, she has health issues—but she is doing it. Her team runs, for the most part, like a well-oiled machine. She gets rides from the local senior service center to all of her appointments. Friends take her to church and out socializing. A man comes every week to read her mail to her and help pay bills. Her aide comes each afternoon to prepare dinner and helps with weekly chores such as laundry, organizing the fridge, and cleaning up. A volunteer for a local caregiver coalition takes her grocery shopping once a week. The hair appointment is on Thursdays. The cleaning woman comes once a month.

It takes a village.

Statistics show that the average yearly cost of an assisted living facility ($49,635) or a nursing home ($131,853) makes these options financially prohibitive for many.[1] The viable alternative is to safely age in place. While much depends on the physical and mental health of the individual, the scope of their care team, and available support services, aging in place can be accomplished at a significantly lower cost. The psychosocial benefits of remaining in their own home, continuing to be socially active in their community, and maintaining established relationships are priceless.

My hope is that *Age in Place: A Guide to Modifying, Organizing, and Decluttering Mom and Dad's Home* will enable you to create a proactive plan to help your parents thrive in their homes for as long as they desire.

Remember, you are not alone. National statistics reveal that over 10,000 people turn 65 years of age every single day,[2] and that 90 percent of them want to stay in their homes indefinitely.[3] It can be done, and the information in this book will lead you on your journey.

Let us know how you are doing. My Facebook page, the Organized Caregiver, is a place to share progress, frustrations, and suggestions as we learn new ideas and garner support. It's there as one more way to keep mom and dad safe—and you sane.

Addendum: It is amazing how long it takes between handing in a manuscript and completing the final edits and revisions. A year actually. Today Billie turned 101 and she is still living in her home. Fiercely independent. Aging in place.

Part 3

Odds and Ends

Resources

The Mother List: Vital Documents You Should Be Able to Locate

Legal:

Last will and testament

Power of attorney

Health care proxy and alternate

Health care directives

Health Care:

Personal medical history (surgeries, immunizations, allergies, blood type, medication list)

Family medical history

Current medical conditions

Doctors/dentist with contact information

Authorizations to release health information

Medicare/Medicaid card

MOLST (medical treatment orders for life-sustaining treatment)

Insurance:

Health insurance policies and cards

Life insurance policies with contact information for beneficiaries

Long-term care policies

Supplemental polices (e.g., Aflac)

Homeowners/renters policies

Auto policies

Identifying Information:

Driver's license or non-driver ID

Social Security number/card

Passport/green card

Vital Records:

Birth certificate

Marriage license

Divorce decree

Military records

Adoption papers

Financial Information:

Name/location of banks with account numbers

Online bank info with user names and passwords

Investment accounts—stocks, bonds, mutual funds

US savings bonds

Name/location of safe deposit box with key and number

Credit/debit card statements/access to actual cards

Retirement accounts—pension, 401(k), IRA, thrift savings plan

Checkbooks/passbooks

Existing loans and balances owed

Tax returns covering the last seven years

Hidden cash, treasures, safes/vaults

Deeds:

House

Car title

Cemetery plot

Any other properties

Household:

Mortgage

Home equity loans

Apartment lease

Property/school tax records

Utility bills—electric, water, gas or oil

Service Providers:

Lawyer

Accountant

Insurance agent

Banker(s)

Stockbroker

Electrician

Plumber

Handyman

Trash removal

Lawn care/snow removal

Deliveries:

Newspapers and magazines

Mail

Post office box location, number, and key

Pet Information:

Veterinarian

Health history

Food type

Career/Personal Highlights (for Obituary):

Employment history and dates

Awards

Honors

Death:

Instructions for funeral

Burial arrangements

What May Be Included in the Health Care Notebook

I. Health History

+ Chronic illnesses, surgical history with dates, acute episodes (broken bones, non-chronic skin issues, etc.)

+ Feminine history (if applicable)

+ Family history (all generations of blood relatives—children, parents, siblings, grandparents, aunts, uncles, and cousins)

II. Insurance Information

+ Photocopy of all relevant cards

+ Policy numbers, ID numbers

+ Contact people, case managers at health insurance agency

III. Diagnostic Tests/Lab Results

+ Written reports of test results and labs with date and doctor who ordered clearly delineated

+ Name, location, contact information for test sites—where tests, films, slides, and other data is stored

IV. Medications

+ Current drugs with dose, frequency, why they were ordered, and when

+ Contact information for doctors who ordered these drugs

+ Pharmacy contact information

V. Treatment Information

- Names of doctors who are currently treating the patient, with all contact information

- Names of therapists, nurses, social workers, and any other ancillary medical personnel, with contact information

- Information/plans regarding current treatments (chemotherapy, home exercise programs, drug regimens, etc.)

VI. Daily Log

- Diary of medical events as they happen—brief entries to help keep a chronological record

VII. Support

- Information regarding various support groups

- Advocates—family members, friends, paid advocates—all with contact information

VIII. Home Care

- Information regarding agencies and personnel

- Medical supplies (walkers, wheelchairs, oxygen, diabetic supplies, adaptive equipment, etc.) with receipts, serial numbers, and other pertinent information

IX. Important Papers

- Advance directives—living will, medical power of attorney, health care proxies

- Copies of authorizations for release of medical information (HIPAA)

- Legal power of attorney

References

Introduction

References

1. AARP, "Livable Communities Baby Boomer Facts and Figures," http://www.aarp.org/livable-communities/info-2014/livable -communities-facts-and-figures.html

Chapter 1: The Exterior

References

1. US Postal Service, "Mailbox Guidelines: Installing a New Mailbox," https://www.usps.com/manage/mailboxes.htm.

Resources

Poles and sticks for walking—For more information on trekking poles, hiking poles, or walking sticks, go to YouTube and search "walking with sticks or poles" for tutorials on how to adjust them and use them to enhance walking. "Poles for Hiking, Trekking, and Walking—Benefits" and "Poles for Balance and Mobility and Walking" by Adventure Buddies are two particularly helpful videos.

Garden kneelers—When purchasing a garden kneeler, be sure it is one that is a combination kneeler and seat. These provide support for back and knees when kneeling, and the frame acts as a rail to push up on when you stand up. When flipped over, it provides a sturdy seat for resting. Check out the one at www.gardeners.com, item #40-008.

Chapter 2: The Entrances and Exits

References

1. Center for Inclusive Design and Environmental Access, "Visitability," http://www.udeworld.com/visitability.html.

2. ADA Compliance Director, "Ramps," http://www.ada-compliance.com/ada-compliance/ada-ramp.

3. To see Bailey opening the door, visit http://otherwisehealthy.com/home-life (and while you are there, please check out my other activities and links to my social media sites).

Resources

Ramps, landings, and other transition products—EZ Access provides many types of portable mobility ramps and accessories (www.ezaccess.com). Safe Path is also known for its wide line of transition products (http://safepathproducts.com).

Chapter 3: The Living Room, Dining Room, and General Living Areas

Resources

Seat lifts—Carex Health Brands (www.carex.com) is a reliable medical equipment company offering several types of seat lifts.

Risedale chairs—The beauty of the Risedale chair is since only the seat cushion lifts, it can be placed right against the wall. They are available in a variety of materials, including brocades, so they will often blend in perfectly with the existing furniture. They help the user to maintain dignity by not looking like a lift chair. Search "Risedale lift chair" for more information or to purchase. "

Chapter 4: The Kitchen

Resources

Cooking tools and utensils—OXO products are dedicated "to providing innovative consumer products that make everyday living easier." They study how people interact with products and then try to improve ease of use through the principles of universal design. Go to www.oxo.com to see their products, as well as a blog full of good tips for making life easier.

Aids for the visually impaired—Hi-Mark pens come in several different colors, most commonly black, white, and orange. Bump Dots also come in black, white, and orange and are available in multiple sizes, depending on what size surface you are placing them on. Both products can be found on Amazon and on websites dedicated to low-vision issues.

Step stools—The Winco Chrome Foot Stool with Safety Bar Hand Rail is my idea of a safe step stool (www.medicalproductsdirect.com/footstepstoo.html). Also check out the Shure-Step stool at https://shure-step.com/. The manufacturer describes this stool as the safest senior step stool in the world, and it certainly has very good safety features.

One-handed kitchen utensils—Rocker knives can be found at most home medical supply websites. I personally like www.easierliving.com, where you can find all types of gadgets for the kitchen and, for that matter, every room in the house. What I especially like about this site is they categorize their items by health condition, locations in the home, and brands. One-handed kitchen aids can also be found at www.alimed.com. AliMed, a provider of medical, health care, and ergonomic products, has been in business as long as I have—and that is very long!

Chapter 5: The Bedrooms

References

1. Mayo Clinic, "Orthostatic Hypotension," http://www.mayoclinic.org/diseases-conditions/orthostatic-hypotension/basics/definition/CON-20031255.

Resources

Mattress aids—The Mattress Genie has an air bladder that lies between the mattress and box spring. With the press of a remote control, it can raise the upper body up to 26 inches high. It is an inexpensive alternative to a hospital bed and fits any size mattress. They run between $130 and $180, depending on the size of the bed. It can be purchased on various websites.

Pivot transfer bars—A useful product when the space is tight next to the bed. It will come in two parts: the pole, which is installed between ceiling and floor, and the bar or grip, which is the part mom would hold on to. Medline sells one, and they are a very reputable medical equipment company. A website catering to seniors called Parent Giving (http://senior-products.parentgiving.com) also offers several different types of these devices at reasonable prices.

Transfer handles—This grab bar for the bed is a handy device that gives the user that little extra something to help get up and down. I recommend the types with two cross bars, as they afford two levels of grip handles for extra leverage. Transfer handles from companies such as AliMed and MTS Medical Supply are reputable, but most brands should do the trick.

Chapter 6: The Bathrooms

References

1. US Department of Justice, "2010 ADA Standards for Accessible Design," https://www.ada.gov/regs2010/2010ADAStandards /2010ADAstandards.htm.

Resources

Modifying a walker—On YouTube, the video "How to Put Wheels on a Walker—Popular Home Medical Equipment" by Home Health PT is a great tutorial on adjusting the legs of a wheeled walker so it will fit through most doorways. So many of my patients never knew this was an option. This trick will buy you around 2 inches of extra clearance. A great #HackforHealthandHome.

Bath lifts—Again on YouTube, search for videos featuring the Bellavita Bath Lift by Drive Medical. There are several demonstrating how the product works. I especially like the one with the lady in the pink bathrobe created by MaxiAids.

Toilet lifts—The Toilevator can be purchased through numerous medical supply companies and health websites. The "Standard" can be used with most basic toilet seats, and the "Grande," which of course costs more, is for larger, elongated toilets.

Toiler paper aids—My patients have had success with the Comfort Wipe Toilet Tissue Aid and the Long Reach Comfort Wipe. Both are easily found online. These not only are effective for those with limited range of motion, but they work well for obese patients who have difficulty reaching behind themselves.

Decorative and combination grab bars—These are not your nana's grab bars. Today, with the universal design movement becoming more prevalent, coupled with consumer desire for elegance and disdain for the institutional look, these products are just the ticket. Great Grabz, Invisia, and Grabcessories are three companies that produce beautiful, upscale, regular grab bars, plus grab bars that combine with towel racks, soap dishes, and toilet paper holders.

Chapter 7: The Stairs, Hallways, Basement, and Laundry

Resources

Stairlifts—There are many reputable companies that manufacture stairlifts. Get quotes from different companies, and read the reviews from people who actually have the one you are considering. Two popular companies are Acorn and Bruno.

Chapter 8: General Tips

References

1. Angela Curl, Jessica Bibbo, and Rebecca Johnson, "Dog Walking: The Human-Animal Bond and Older Adults' Physical Health," *Gerontologist*, vol. 57, No. 5, October 2017, 930–939, https://academic.oup.com/gerontologist/article/57/5/930 /2632039/Dog-Walking-the-Human-Animal-Bond-and-Older -Adults.

The results of this study by Rebecca Johnson, director of the Research Center for Human Animal Interaction at the University of Missouri, provided evidence for the association between dog walking and improved physical health using a large, national representative sample. She noted that "animals provide focus, a reason to get up in the morning, an opportunity to exercise, unconditional love, and a social lubricant." Research has shown that pet owners take better care of themselves, rebound faster from illness, and have lower blood pressure and incidents of heart disease.

2. Centers for Disease Control and Prevention, "Nonfatal Fall-Related Injuries Associated with Dogs and Cats—United States, 2001–2006," https://www.cdc.gov/mmwr/preview/mmwrhtml/mm5811a1.htm.

The CDC analyzed data from the National Electronic Injury Surveillance System All Injury Program (NEISS-AIP) for the period 2001–2006. Nearly 88 percent of injuries were associated with dogs, and among persons injured, females were 2.1 times more likely to be injured than males.

Resources

Home monitoring systems—There are numerous companies that provide a wide variety of services, including monitoring activity and medication, preventing wandering, and creating an online care portal for the resident and family to interact with each other. Systems that some of my patients have used include Silver Mother (https://sen.se/silvermother), Grand Care Systems (www.grandcare.com), and Philips Lifeline (www.lifeline .philips.com).

Chapter 9: Do Mom and Dad Need Help?

References

1. AARP, "Livable Communities Baby Boomer Facts and Figures," http://www.aarp.org/livable-communities/info-2014/livable -communities-facts-and-figures.html.

2. N. R. Nicholson, "A Review of Social Isolation: An Important but Underassessed Condition in Older Adults," *Journal of Primary Prevention* 33, June 2012, (2–3): 137–52, https://www.ncbi.nlm.nih .gov/pubmed/22766606.

Chapter 10: You Finished the Walk, Now Have the Talk

References

1. Family Caregiver Alliance/National Center on Caregiving, www.caregiver.org. Go to "Caregiver Education," then click on "Fact and Tip Sheets," then click on "Holding a Family Meeting."

Resources

Speaking with your parents—The Conversation Project is a not-for-profit organization that encourages people to talk about their wishes for end-of-life care and provides them with tools to make the conversation easier (www.theconversationproject.org). They believe the place to begin to talk about these important subjects is "at the kitchen table, not the intensive care unit, with people we love before it's too late."

Chapter 11: Form the Team and Prepare to Care

References

1. Patrick Roden, "Aging in Place and Environmental Press," http://aginginplace.com/aging-in-place-and-environmental-press.

2. Family Caregiver Alliance/National Center on Caregiving, https://www.caregiver.org/national-center-caregiving. Go to "Caregiver Education," then click on "Fact and Tip Sheets," then click on "Caregiving with Your Siblings."

3. Aging Life Care Association, http://www.aginglifecare.org.

4. Alzheimer's Association, https://www.alz.org.

5. National Association of Letter Carriers (NALC), https://www.nalc .org/community-service/carrier-alert.

Resources

Creating a health care notebook—See page 170

Chapter 12: Organize and Assign the Tasks—Share the Care
References

1. Lars Osterberg and Terrence Blaschke, "Adherence to Medication," *New England Journal of Medicine*, August 4, 2005, 353, 487–497, http://www.nejm.org/doi/full/10.1056/NEJMra050100.

2. AARP, "Medicines Made Easy: Things You Need to Know About Managing Your Medicines but Were Afraid to Ask, http://assets .aarp.org/www.aarp.org_/articles/health/images/meds/meds _made_easy.pdf.

3. American Association of Daily Money Managers, http://aadmm. com.

Resources

Senior driving—Visit http://seniordriving.aaa.com. Sponsored by AAA, this website has the mission to help senior drivers "drive longer and safer." It provides various information on the physical and cognitive changes we undergo that may affect driving, how to evaluate driving ability, tips for improving driving ability, and resources for caregivers.

Conclusion
References

1. Genworth, "Compare Long-Term Care Costs Across the United States," https://www.genworth.com/about-us/industry-expertise /cost-of-care.html.

The Genworth "Cost of Care" survey has been used for long-term care planning since 2004. The 2016 survey was conducted by Carescout. The numbers quoted in the book were the median for New York State and vary depending on location. Go to the website and enter your own state to help with your future planning.

2. Pew Research Center, "Baby Boomers Retire," December 29, 2010, http://www.pewresearch.org/daily-number/baby-boomers-retire.

3. AARP, "Livable Communities Baby Boomer Facts and Figures," http://www.aarp.org/livable-communities/info-2014/livable-communities-facts-and-figures.html.

Other Resources

Age in Place at Home (www.aipathome.com)—This website is focused on providing information to help people age in place by "showing the benefits of using universal design, telecare technologies, and other assistive products to make life easier." There are great videos, pictures, and tutorials on everything you need to know to make modifications.

Aids for Arthritis (www.aidsforarthritis.com, toll-free phone: 1-800-654-0707)—Great variety of gadgets and equipment for people having difficulty with ADLs and IADLs.

AARP (www.aarp.org; toll-free phone: 1-888-OUR-AARP, 1-888-687-2277; toll-free Spanish phone: 1-877-342-2277)—AARP provides tool kits and fact sheets on aging in place and caregiving.

Eldercare Locator (www.eldercare.gov, toll-free phone: 1-800-677-1116)—This is a nationwide public service of the Administration on Aging and the US Department of Health and Human Services that connects you to services for older adults and their caregivers. This is a fantastic website. You only need to enter your zip code or city and it will generate lists with complete contact information on everything you need to know to help your loved one live independently in their community.

Elderluxe (www.elderluxe.com)—This is a fun website that has high-end luxury items for health and the home. It includes mobility aids, adaptive equipment, and electronic and fitness items. I'm particularly fond of the walking cane encrusted with Swarovski crystals.

Lotsa Helping Hands (http://lotsahelpinghands.com)—This site talks you through the steps of organizing a care community by setting up a web-based calendar with all the information needed to help mom and dad stay home. It also facilitates the creation of a health care notebook and organizes helpers for such things as meals, rides to appointments, personal care, and home management.

National Alliance for Caregiving (www.caregiving.org, 301-718-8444)— This is a coalition of national organizations that focus on advancing family caregiving. Their mission is to improve the quality of life for families and their care recipients through research, innovation, and advocacy.

National Association of Home Builders (www.NAHB.com, toll-free phone: 800-368-5242)—They will provide a list of certified aging-in-place specialists in your area.

Focusheets

The following Focusheets® (fill-in-the-blank worksheets) are designed to help you assess various aspects of your home when you complete a thorough walk-through. You need not fill in every little blank; instead use these guides to help you focus on things you may not normally be aware of. You will also find tips, taken from the various chapters, which will serve as quick reminders of the ideal conditions for safety and ease in navigating throughout the house.

Keep Mom and Dad Safe   Exterior, Entranceway, and Garage Focusheet

Driveway	Type: _____ Condition: _____ Lighting: _____
Sidewalk	Type: _____ Condition: _____ Lighting: _____
Lawn	Condition: (Describe topography - flat, hilly, dips, etc.) _____ _____ _____
Steps to front door	Number _____ Height/Rise _____ (Minimum rise of 4″ max 7¾″ high; Tread depth 11″) Type/Condition: _____
Railings	One side _____ Both sides _____ Type: _____ (Ideally railings extend beyond top and bottom steps) Condition: _____
Porch or landing	Condition: _____ Lighting _____
Exterior lighting	Above door _____ Wall sconce _____ Motion sensors _____ Other exterior (Detail) _____
Front door area	Width _____ (Ideal 36″ wide) Knob/Lever _____ Peephole _____ Side window _____ Easy lock _____ Accessible door bell _____ (Ideally lighted) Welcome mat _____ (Ideally large, heavy but not thick) Entranceway covered or uncovered _____ (Ideally a covered entranceway)

Front door threshold	Description: _____ _____ (Ideally no more that 1/2" high beveled threshold)
Visibility/ Access	House number clearly visible from the street _____ Emergency exit plan _____ _____ (Role play with them)
Back door area	Width _____ Knob/Lever _____ Easy lock _____ Threshold _____ Back steps _____ (If applicable - ideally with railings)
Garage	Unattached _____ Is the pathway/walkway to house clear? _____ Is there adequate lighting? _____ Attached _____ Entrance to house: Ground level _____ Below level _____ How many steps? _____ Is there a railing? _____ Type: One/two car _____ Is the garage cluttered? _____ Are pathways clear? _____ Is there extra space for storage? _____
Miscellaneous	Mailbox location: On house _____ End of driveway _____ Where are garbage cans kept/must they be taken out to: _____

Keep Mom and Dad Safe   **Living Room Focusheet**

Doorway width _____ (32" min/36" ideally) Flooring type _____
(Ideally flat/no change in surface; If carpet less than 1/2" pile ideal)
Potentially hazardous throw rug _____ Pathway accessibility _____
Hallway width _____ (36" min)
Threshold into room _____ (Ideally no more that 1/4")
Is the room on the same level or sunken? _____

Lighting: Overhead _____ Furniture lamps _____
Overhead fan/light _____
Position of light switches _____
(Rocker/touch switches are best; 42"–48" up from the floor)
Accessibility of electrical outlets _____ (Ideally 15" up from the floor)

Furniture and accessibility _____

_____
(Ideally the higher and firmer the easier to get on and off. Best to be arranged so
there are clear pathways to couch and chairs)
Description of pieces/furniture height _____

_____

Telephone accessibility _____ (Ideally cordless phone
with bases and headsets in bedroom, kitchen and living room/den)
Location of wire and cords _____
Cellular phone _____

Are windows accessible? _____ (Ideally easy to open, close, lock, and manage
window treatments)
Type of windows _____
Type of window treatments _____

Keep Mom and Dad Safe　　　　　　　　　**Dining Room Focusheet**

Doorway width _____ (32" min/36" ideally) Flooring type _____

(Ideally flat/no change in surface; If carpet less than 1/2" pile ideal)

Potentially hazardous throw rug _____ Pathway accessibility _____

Hallway width _____ (36" min)

Threshold into room _____ (Ideally no more that 1/4")

Lighting: Overhead _____ Furniture lamps _____

Overhead fan/light _____

Position of light switches _____

(Rocker/touch switches are best; 42"–48" up from the floor)

Accessibility of electrical outlets _____(Ideally 15" up from the floor)

Is there sufficient room to navigate around the dining room table? _____

Is there at least one arm chair? _____

Are windows accessible? _____ (Ideally easy to open, close, lock, and manage

window treatments)

Type of windows _____

Type of window treatments _____

187

Keep Mom and Dad Safe   Family Room/Den Focusheet

Doorway width _____ (32" min/36" ideally) Flooring type _____

(ideally flat/no change in surface; If carpet less than 1/2" pile ideal)

Potentially hazardous throw rug _____ Pathway accessibility _____

Hallway width _____ (36" min)

Threshold into room _____ (ideally no more that 1/4")

Is the room on the same level or sunken? _____

Lighting: Overhead _____ Furniture lamps _____

Overhead fan/light _____

Position of light switches _____

(Rocker/touch switches are best; 42"–48" up from the floor)

Accessibility of electrical outlets _____ (ideally 15" up from the floor)

Furniture and accessibility _____

_____

(Ideally the higher and firmer the easier to get on and off. Best to be arranged so

there are clear pathways to couch and chairs)

Description of pieces/furniture height _____

_____

Telephone accessibility _____ (Ideally cordless phone

with bases and headsets in bedroom, kitchen and living room/den)

Location of wire and cords _____

Cellular phone _____

Are windows accessible? _____ (Ideally easy to open, close, lock, and manage

window treatments)

Type of windows _____

Type of window treatments _____

Keep Mom and Dad Safe   Office/Study Focusheet

Doorway width _____ (32" min/36" ideally) Flooring type _____

(ideally flat/no change in surface; If carpet less than 1/2" pile ideal)

Potentially hazardous throw rug _____ Pathway accessibility _____

Hallway width _____ (36" min)

Threshold into room _____ (ideally no more that 1/4")

Is the room on the same level or sunken? _____

Lighting: Overhead _____ Furniture lamps _____

Overhead fan/light _____

Position of light switches _____

(Rocker/touch switches are best; 42"–48" up from the floor)

Accessibility of electrical outlets _____(ideally 15" up from the floor)

Furniture and accessibility _____

_____

(Ideally the higher and firmer the easier to get on and off. Best to be arranged so

there are clear pathways to couch and chairs)

Description of pieces/furniture height _____

_____

Telephone accessibility _____ (Ideally cordless phone

with bases and headsets in bedroom, kitchen and living room/den)

Location of wire and cords _____

Cellular phone _____

Are windows accessible? _____ (Ideally easy to open, close, lock, and manage

window treatments)

Type of windows _____

Type of window treatments _____

Keep Mom and Dad Safe   **Kitchen Focusheet**

Counter height _____ (Ideally 34"–36" high)

Flooring type _____ (Ideally slip resistant)

Room lighting _____

Workspace lighting _____

(Ideally over the sink, stove and food preparation areas)

Refrigerator/Freezer type _____ (easiest access is side by side)

Oven type - gas or electric_____ (Ideally 18" off the floor)

Position of cooktop controls _____ (Ideally in front)

Microwave location _____ (Ideally adjacent to a heat resistant

countertop/shelf)

Accessibility of cabinets _____ (Ideally "D" shaped handles)

Accessibility of shelving _____

Accessibility of electrical outlets _____ (Place power strip on

counter if needed)

Sink/Faucet type _____(Ideally a single lever faucet)

Fire extinguisher - Make sure it covers different types of fires _____

Location(s) _____

Configuration: Draw layout of the kitchen. Ideally good to have 18"–24" of a cleared

countertop space next to the oven, cooktop, microwave and sink.

Are open spaces wide enough for a wheelchair - 5 foot diameter? _____

If a galley kitchen, can they hold onto the counters? _____

Is the table easily accessible? _____ Do kitchen chairs have arms? _____

(Ideally easily to transfer in and out of an armchair. If need be borrow one from

another room and bring it in.)

Keep Mom and Dad Safe	**Bedroom Focusheet**

Location of bedroom _____ Doorway width _____

Flooring type _____

Pathways - cluttered or uncluttered? _____

(Pathways ideally clear - especially to the bathroom)

Lighting: Overhead _____ Night table lamps _____ (Ideally easily accessible from bed)

Overhead fan/light _____ Nightlight _____

Bed type/size _____ Height of bed _____ (Ideally 22" high from floor to top of mattress)

Do they sleep in the bed? _____ Can they easily get on to the bed? _____

Does the bed need to be moved to improve bedroom access/mobility? _____

Does the bedspread present a potential tripping hazard? _____

List other furniture in the room _____

_____

(Ideally including an arm chair to sit on for dressing)

Is the furniture arranged to allow for clear, unobstructed pathways? _____

Is the night stand height comparable to the bed? _____

Will moving the bed closer to the night stand improve accessibility? _____

Telephone type (corded-uncorded)/Location _____

Is the closet easily accessible? _____

Closet rod/shelving accessibility _____

Is there lighting in the closet? _____

Are windows accessible? _____ (Ideally easy to open, close, lock, and manage window treatments)

Type of windows _____

Type of window treatments _____

Keep Mom and Dad Safe   **Bathroom Focusheet**

Doorway width _____ (ideally 36″) Turning radius in bathroom _____

Lighting: Overhead _____ Wall _____ Vanity _____

Accessibility/Location of electrical outlets _____

Flooring/Condition _____

Sink height _____ (Ideally 30″–34″ to top of the vanity)

Type of sink _____ (Pedestal vs. Cabinet)

Faucet type _____ (Ideally single lever)

Toilet height from floor _____ (Ideally 17″–19″)

Side clearance _____ Shape of toilet bowl: Oblong _____ Round _____

If full bath: Shower Accessibility: Glass door _____ Curtain _____

Faucet type _____ Wall Surface (tile/fiberglass/other) _____

Grab bar(s)_____ Shower seat _____ Flooring/condition _____

Shower mat _____ Lighting in/over shower _____

If full bath: Bathtub accessibility: Glass door _____ Curtain _____

Wall height to enter _____ Faucet type _____

Wall surface (tile/fiberglass/other) _____ Tub seat _____

Grab bar type/location _____

Flooring type/condition _____

Bath mat condition _____ Lighting over tub _____

Keep Mom and Dad Safe	Stairways, Hallways, Basement, and Laundry Room Focusheet
Main stairway	Number of steps _____ (ideally risers max 7" high/tread 11" deep) Stairway width _____ Lighting switches Bottom: _____ Top: _____ (ideally switches at bottom and top) Railing length _____ (Ideally extended beyond top and bottom steps; 1¼"–1½" round for ease of grip; 1½" away from the wall) One or both sides _____
Stairway flooring	Wood _____ Carpet _____ Concrete _____ Other _____ Condition: _____
Other stairways	Basement/Attic: Location in house _____ Number of steps _____ Height of steps _____ Type/Condition: _____ _____
Hallways	Width _____ (Ideally 36" wide) Flooring type _____ Lighting/Switches _____ (Ideally switches on either end of hallway)
Basement	Type of flooring _____ Lighting _____ Finished basement? _____
Laundry room	Location _____ (if in basement, detail stairway based on above questions) _____ _____ Doorway width _____ Flooring type _____ Pathways - clear or cluttered? _____ Washer type _____ (Ideally front loading) Accessibility _____ Dryer type _____ Accessibility _____ Shelving/Cabinet type and height _____ _____

Index